THE
GARDENER'S
Perpetual Almanack

MARTIN HOYLES

THE
GARDENER'S
Perpetual Almanack

A BOOK OF DAYS
with 233 illustrations, 54 in colour

THAMES AND HUDSON

For our daughter Rosa with love

Cover illustration: J. Gesner, *Triandria,* from *Tabulae Phytographicae* 1795–1804. By courtesy of the Board of Trustees of the Victoria and Albert Museum.

Grateful acknowledgment is made for permission to use extracts from the following:
Louise Beebe Wilder, *Adventures in a a Suburban Garden,* Macmillan Inc, New York. Alice Coats, *The Book of Flowers,* © 1973 by Phaidon Press Limited. Blanche Henrey, *British Botanical and Horticultural Literature before 1800,* 1975, by permission of Oxford University Press. Gertrude Jekyll, *Colour in the Flower Garden,* now published by The Antique Collector's Club as *Colour Schemes for the Flower Garden. Country Notes* copyright 1939 Vita Sackville-West, reproduced by permission of Curtis Brown, London. *Derek Jarman's Garden,* Derek Jarman, with photographs by Howard Sooley, published by Thames and Hudson, © 1995 Estate of Derek Jarman. Harold Nicolson, *Diaries 1939-1945,* HarperCollins *Publishers* Limited. Edward Hyams, *English Cottage Gardens,* Whittet Books, London. *The Englishman's Flora,* David Higham Associates and Geoffrey Grigson. *Flowers and their Histories,* A & C Black and Alice Coats. Clare Leighton, *Four Hedges,* by kind permission of David Leighton. Karel Capek, *The Gardener's Year,* George Allen & Unwin, an imprint of HarperCollins *Publishers* Limited. Patience Strong, *The Glory of the Garden,* by kind permission of her Literary Trustee and Rupert Crew Ltd.

Eleanor Perenyi, *Green Thoughts,* Random House, New York. Agnes Arber, *Herbals,* 1912, Cambridge University Press. Mary Thorne Quelch, *Herbs for Daily Use,* Faber and Faber Ltd as Publishers. E.H.M. Cox, *A History of Gardening in Scotland,* Chatto & Windus. *In Your Garden* copyright 1951 Vita Sackville-West, reproduced by permission of Curtis Brown, London. *In Your Garden,* Percy Thrower and Reed Books. Mrs M. Grieve and Hilda Leyel, *A Modern Herbal,* Jonathan Cape. Maude Haworth-Booth *My Garden Diary,* John Murray (Publishers) Ltd. Alice Sloane Anderson (ed.) *Our Garden Heritage,* Dodd, Mead & Company, New York. Copyright by The Garden Club of America. Eleanour Sinclair Rohde, *The Scented Garden* and *Shakespeare's Wild Flowers,* The Medici Society Limited, London. Edward Anson, *The Small Garden,* John Murray (Publishers) Ltd. Sam Bass Warner, Jr. *To Dwell is to Garden: A History of Boston's Community Gardens.* Copyright 1987 by Sam Bass Warner, Jr. Reprinted with permission of Northeastern University Press. Balmori and Morton, *Transitory Gardens, Uprooted Lives,* © 1993 by Yale University. Margery Fish, *We Made a Garden,* Mitchell Beazley Publishers (1995), reprinted by permission of Reed International Books. Text © Lesley Ann Boyd-Carpenter.

Every effort has been made to trace the copyright holders of material quoted, and any omissions are regretted.

British Library Cataloguing-in-Publication Data
A catalogue record for this book is available from the British Library

ISBN 0-500-01763-8

Printed and bound in Slovenia by Mladinska Knjiga

Foreword

In the decay of the moon,
A cloudy morning bodes a fair afternoon.
Old English Proverb

The Almanack, next to the 'One Great Book', is most indispensable.
John Almond *The Almanack* 1911

The Gardener's Perpetual Almanack draws on the wit and wisdom of over four
centuries of almanacks and gardening books to provide a wealth of advice
and inspiration for all gardeners. There are vivid quotations for every day
of the year, and gardening tips old and new, such as how to fertilize peaches
with a rabbit's tail or get rid of moles, when to plant potatoes or establish an
apiary, and how to make compost or use ashes from the bonfire.

The Saxons carved the moon cycles for the year on a square stick of
wood, called *al-mon-aght* ('all moon-heed'), but our word almanack seems
more likely to have come from the Arabic *Al Manack*, meaning 'the Diary'.
Traditionally almanacks contained a calendar of the months and days of the
year, with the dates of fasts, holidays, saints' days and other festivals. They
recorded the risings and settings of the sun and the moon and the rotation
of the stars, and they made predictions about the weather. They often also
gave advice on gardening and husbandry, and herbal cures and recipes. Over
two thousand different almanacks were published in the seventeenth century,
and one sold more than sixteen thousand copies each year between 1646 and
1648, over twelve times as many as another seventeenth-century bestseller,
Milton's *Paradise Lost*.

The Gardener's Perpetual Almanack is meant to be enjoyed year after year, so
does not include the phases of the moon. For centuries, however, it was

believed that the moon and planets influenced the growth of plants. Before 1700 and the Age of Reason, astrology was a respectable science, although there were early sceptics, such as the Puritan William Fulke, one of the founders of scientific meteorology in England, who said in 1566 :

> Good days to sowe and plante, I thinke be when the earth
> is moderately moystened, and gentilly warmed with the heate
> of the sonne. As for the sygne or constellation, it is as muche
> healpe unto the sedes as it was ease for the Camell whenne
> the Flye leapt of from his backe.

For Francis Bacon, William Harvey, Nicholas Culpeper and other scientific thinkers of the seventeenth century, astrology was an attempt to explain cause and effect by physical rather than metaphysical means. In contrast, when the reactionary Royalist William Coles attacked the radical Parliamentarian Culpeper in his *Art of Simpling* in 1656, he did not present scientific evidence to disprove the claims for astrological botany, but appealed to the authority of the Bible, arguing that, since God created the plants before the stars, they could not be influenced by the heavenly bodies.

By 1694, however, Robert Sharrock was representative of a general change of view on astrology: 'I prescribe nothing concerning the observation of the faces of the Moon; For though the Moon hath greater influence upon all terrestrial bodies, than any other Planet, except the Sun, yet I cannot think it is much Material under what Phase of the Moon the Gardiner either Sows or Plants.' Belief in astrology was often ridiculed, as in *Poor Robin's Almanac for the Year 1805*, published in Philadelphia: 'Any time in the month of March is a proper season to prune your trees: mind nothing about the moon, for she concerns herself little about you or your trees, and the sign is always in the right place when it makes you industrious.'

Nevertheless the belief in astrology has never completely died out. Fanny Bergen at the close of the nineteenth century stresses the importance of the almanack among farming communities in the USA:

> These superstitions regarding planting crops according to the
> moon are by no means idle sayings that have no influence over
> farmers. I know positively that in many parts of the United
> States and in Prince Edward Island gardens and fields are often
> planted after direct reference to the almanac in regard to the
> moon's changes.

Even throughout this century belief in the influence of the moon persists. Bruce Blunt records in *Radishes to Roses* (1936): 'I know several gardeners – men of long experience and wide knowledge, successful exhibitors at great shows, well abreast of modern developments – who would never dream of sowing their seeds at the waning of the moon if they could possibly avoid it.' And in 1952 Geoffrey Grigson writes in *Gardenage*: 'I know at least one clever gardener who always plants peas while the moon is waxing.' In the French *Almanach du Vieux Savoyard* for 1996 there is a section for gardeners who wish to plant according to the phases of the moon.

By the nineteenth century, British almanacks included all sorts of extra information, such as weights and measures, the distances between towns, high tides, details of fairs, new books and lists of Members of Parliament. Gardening almanacks contained details of horticultural societies, lists of new flowers and information about the laws relating to gardens and the theft of plants. Writing in the first half of the nineteenth century, John Clare, the Northamptonshire poet and gardener, tells in *The Shepherd's Calendar* of a farmer sitting reading either the news:

> Or old Moore's annual prophecies
> Of flooded fields and clouded skies;
> Whose Almanac's thumb'd pages swarm
> With frost and snow, and many a storm,
> And wisdom, gossip'd from the Stars,
> Of politics and bloody wars.
> He shakes his head, and still proceeds,
> Nor doubts the truth of what he reads:
> All wonders are with faith supplied –
> Bible, at once, and weather-guide.

Many comic almanacks were published during the first half of the nineteenth century, whose origins can be seen in the seventeenth-century *Poor Robin's Almanack* and the American *Poor Richard's Almanack* from the eighteenth century. Political, religious and military almanacks also became the vogue. *The People's Calendar* (1892), for example, supported the Liberal Party and Labour, campaigning for 'home rule for villages, the restoration of common lands and the right of the people to game thereon, free education, the promotion of Trade Unions and shorter hours of labour'.

In *The Gardener's Perpetual Almanack,* each month opens with an explanation of its name, taken from *The North American Almanac for 1775* by

Samuel Stearns. There are also figures for temperature and rainfall from Sutton's *Gardener's Calendar for 1885*; they represent the average temperature over forty-two years and the average rainfall over sixty-eight years, as measured at the Greenwich Observatory (the metric equivalents are given in brackets).

Each date has its own plant name (though a few plants are revisited on different dates). These are from Mrs Wirt's *Flora's Dictionary* of 1855, based on those in *The Every-Day Book* by William Hone, printed in London in 1826, in their turn taken from traditional calendars of saints' days and their plants. Some botanical names do not accord with modern usage, so, for instance, *Hyacinthus nonscriptus* (the flower for 23 April) is given for the harebell, now strictly used for the bluebell, and *Campanula rotundifolia* (4 August) is given for the bluebell, nowadays used for the harebell (the bluebell of Scotland).

For every day of the year there is also a short piece of seasonal advice or information, taken from old almanacks and gardening books, and a gardening quotation or two – some wise, some lyrical, some very funny, many from the greatest writers in the English language. Several are from books on the language of flowers popular in the nineteenth century, ascribing different meanings to different flowers. The idea, based on a Turkish tradition, first appeared in a French book published in Paris in 1818, from which the many English works are derived.

Much of the advice given is still relevant today, though some must be taken with a pinch of salt. Gardeners must also remember that before 1752 the 'Old Style' or 'Julian' calendar was in use, every succeeding year lagging further behind the solar year. Britain finally decided to come into line with the rest of Europe in 1752, and suddenly 3 September became 14 September. Clearly eleven days can make a crucial difference for a gardener: for instance, birds and blossoms traditionally expected on 1 May are more likely to appear towards the middle of the month. And it seems that global warming will have to be taken into account as it affects the seasonal traditions in the gardener's calendar.

> Let the gardener, then, read this book with a diligent eye for such advice and suggestions as he can apply to his own problems, but without any attempt to follow it blindly: for the real work, like the profit there may be (ten dimes saved is a dollar earned!), and the pleasure there is sure to be, must belong to the gardener, and cannot be put between the covers of a book.
> Frederick Frye Rockwell *Around the Year in the Garden* 1917

Sources of Illustrations

Arabic numerals refer to days of the month, Roman to the months:
Anonymous 11/XII. Arcimboldo 10/I. C. Aubriet
25/XII. H. Avercamp 16/XII. O. Beert the Elder 3/IX.
H. Bol & A. Collaert 10/IX. J. Bradick 13/IV. P. Brueghel
II 31/III. D.Burroughs 17/VI. Cambridge: Fitzwilliam
Museum 7/III. Charlottesville, Virginia: Thomas Jefferson
Memorial Foundation Inc. 13/IV. G. Cibo 26/IV. E. de
Critz 4/VIII. W. Dilley 11/XI. G. D. Ehret 16/II 1/V
21/XI 6/XII. N. d'Esménard 7/III. Florence: Gabinetto
Disegni e Stampe degli Uffizi 23/VIII; Pitti Palace 29/II,
Scala 30/V 23/VIII. C. D. Friedrich 8/VI. G. Garzoni
29/II. J. de Gheyn 22/IV. Grandville 18/II 13/III 20/VI
27/VI. A. Van Henstenburg 25/VII 26/VII 27/VII.
E. Hodgkin 27/III 30/IX 30/X 17/XI 30/XII. W. Hollar
5/I 17/I 14/IV 18/V 29/V 17/VIII. R. de Hooghe,
Harrewijn 13/X. Kew: by courtesy of the Royal Botanic
Gardens 24/VIII 24/X. N. de Larmessin frontispiece,
10/X. Clare Leighton wood engravings (by permission of
David Leighton) 26/III 12/VII 28/X. J. Ligozzi 23/VIII.
London: Aldus Archive, titlepage, 13/VIII 17/IX 8/XII;
by permission of the British Library 12/I 27/II 26/IV 7 &
8/V 19/VII 7/XI, copyright British Museum 1/IX;
Photograph Christie's 31/III; Courtesy Simon Finch Rare
Books 1/III 10/III 11/III 12/III 28/III 22/IX 23/IX
11/X 24/XI 24/XII; photographs courtesy Hazlitt,
Gooden & Fox 27/III 30/IX 30/X 17/XI 30/XII;
photographs courtesy John Mitchell & Son 6/II 16/III
25/VII 26/VII 27/VII 3/IX; William Morris Gallery
3/VI; The Natural History Museum 21/V; Phillips Fine
Art Auctioneers 21/XI; Royal Horticultural Society,
Lindley Library 6/VI 11/XII 22/XII; Courtesy Henry
Sotheran Limited 26/V 31/V 29/VI 5/VII 23/X;
Courtesy of the Board of Trustees of the Victoria and
Albert Museum 17/III 1/V 26/X 6/XII. F. Lutyens
29/XI. C. P. Marillier 16/VII. Photo K. Markham 1/III
10/III 11/III 12/III 28/III 26/V 31/V 29/VI 5/VIII
22/IX 23/IX 11/X 23/X 2/XI 24/XI 24/XII. D. Martin
22/XII. A. McCullum 27/XI. M. S. Merian 21/II 14/V.
W. Morris 3/VI. J. Le Moyne de Morgues 11/III 16/VIII
1/IX 26/X. Nottingham Castle Museum 21/II. K. Ogilvy
endpapers, 13/IX. Oxford: Ashmolean Museum 4/VIII;
By courtesy of the Bodleian Library 31/VIII. L. Palermo
16/III. Paris: Bibliothèque Nationale 25/V 20/X; Institut
Néerlandais, Fondation Custodia 22/IV. Pompeii: Casa
del Bracciale d'Oro 30/V. Private Collections 1/III 10/III
11/III 12/III 27/III 28/III 5/IV 14/V 9/VII 22/IX
23/IX 30/IX 11/X 30/X 2/XI 17/XI 24/XI 24/XII
30/XII. M. A. Raimondi 9/I. P.-J. Redouté 6/II 14/VII.
N. Robert & N. Jarry 31/XII. T. Robins 5/IV. Rome:
Biblioteca Casanatense 2/V 1/VII. The Toledo Museum
of Art, Ohio 16/XII. Vienna: Österreichs National-
bibliothek 8/IV. M. de Vos & N. de Bruyn 22/III, & A.
Collaert 14/II 24/VII 19/IX 1/XII, & C. de Passe 25/IV
20/IX. H. Vredeman de Vries 9/VII. A. I. Withers 6/VI.
Books: R. Bewick *History of British Birds* (1797–1804)
25/I. E. Blackwell *A Curious Herbal* (1737) 15/III, and
Herbarium (1754–73) 24/VI. H. Bock *Kreuter Buch* (1546)
4/I 11/VI 2/X. *The Book of Medecine* (1557) 29/X. *The
Botanical Magazine* (1832) 24/VIII. O. Brunfels *Herbarium
viva eicones* (1532) 2/II. J. T. de Bry *Florilegium Novum*
(1612) 25/VI. *Camerarius Florilegium* (c.1590) 6/III.
H. Cause *De koninglycke hovenier* (1676) 29/IV.
J. Commelijn *Horti medici* (1697–1701) 6/IV, and

Nederlantze Hesperides (1676) 23/IV. W. Curtis *Flora
Londinensis* (1777-98) 3/XI, and *The Flower Garden Displayed*
7/VII. T. Delord *Les fleurs animées* (1859) 18/II 13/III
20/VI 27/VI. A. Dietrich *Flora regni Borussici* (1832–44)
18/XI. R. Dodoens *Stirpium Historiæ Pemptades Sex* (1583)
3/V. *Een Hondert Emblematas* (1624–26) 27/I 2/IX 8/X.
H. L. Duhamel du Monceau *Traité des arbres fruitiers* (1768).
J. Evelyn *Silva* (1776) 13/I 25/IX. R. Fludd *Medicina
Catholica* (1629) 12/XI. L. Fuchs *De historia stirpium* (1542)
26/I 23/II 14/VIII. R. Furber *Catalogue of Garden Produce
and Flowers* (1732) 3/X, and *Twelve Months of Flowers* (1730)
plate for each month. J. Gerard *The Herball* (1597) 30/III
23/X, (1636) 15/I 26/II 17/VII. J. Gesner *Tabulae
Phytographicae* (1795–1804) 31/I. W. Good *Garden Work*
(1915) 6/VII 7/X 4/XI. J. R. Green *Short History of the
English People* (1898) 13/VI. T. Green *Universal Herbal*
(1820) 22/VIII. M. Harris *The Aurelian or Natural History
of English Moths and Butterflies* (1840) 29/VI 5/VII.
C. Hindley *A History of the Cries of London* (1885) 12/VI
3/XII. W. H. von Hohberg *Georgica Curiosa* (1658) 2/I
11/II 22/II 22/V 27/V 31/VII 26/IX 6/X 14/X 20/XI
19/XII. W. Hone *The Every-day Book* (1831) 14/IX.
J. D. Hooker *The Rhododendrons of Sikkim-Himalaya* (1849)
26/V. *Hortus Sanitatis* (1491) 9/II 1/III 10/III 11/III
12/III 28/III 14/VI 22/IX 23/IX 11/X 2/XI 24/XI
24/XII. J. J. Huggelin *Von heilsamen Baedern* (1559)
28/VIII. *The Illustrated London News* 21 Dec. 1850 16/I.
J. Jacóps *Citricultura* (1682) 7/XII. N. J. Jacquin *Hortus
botanicus Vindobonensis* (1770–76) 4/VIII. W. Jardine *British
Birds* 2/IV. V. J. von Krombholz *Naturgetreue Abbildungen*
(1831–46) 19/X. W. Lawson *A New Orchard and Garden*
(1618) 19/III. L. Liger *La nouvelle maison rustique* (1749)
22/I. Mrs. Loudon *The Ladies' Flower Garden* (1841) 3/V.
M. Maryon *How the Garden Grew* (1900) 30/I. P. A. Mattioli
Commentarii (1565) 22/XI, and *Herbarz ginak Bylinar* (1562)
2/VI M S Merian *Florilegium Renovatum et Auctum* (1641)
2/VII, and *Der Raupen wunderbare Verwandelung* (1679)
24/III 30/VII. P. A. Micheli *Nova Plantarum Genera* (1729)
5/IX. J. Miller *Illustratio systematis sexualis Linnaei* (1804)
25/VIII. W. Morris *News from Nowhere* (1892) 18/VI.
Didymus Mountaine (T. Hyll) *The Gardener's Labyrinth*
(1638) 28/XII. J. Parkinson *Paradisus* (1629) 12/II 18/IV
19/IV 16/V 12/XII. C. de Passe the Elder *Hortus Floridus:
Altera Pars* (1614) 3/VIII. C. de Passe the Younger *Hortus
Floridus* (1614) 7/II 9/IV. A. Pratt *Our Native Songsters*
(1857) 23/XI. J. de la Quintinie *Instructions pour les Jardins*
(1692) 10/IV. J. Rasch *Weinbuch* (1582) 9/IX.
P.-J. Redouté *Choix des Plus Belles Fleurs* (1827) 23/VI. *Le
Roman de la Rose* (1494–95) 22/VII. J.-J. Rousseau *Emile*
(1785) 16/VII. J. Sannazaro *Arcadia* (1510) 15/VI. S. Serlio
Tutte l'opere d'architettura et prospettiva (1619) 19/I. Society of
Gardeners *Catalogus Plantarum* (1730) 1/IV 27/VII.
W. Strabo *Hortulus* (1512) 2/III 16/XI. W. Swaysland
Familiar Wild Birds (1883) 7/I. E. Topsell *The History of
Four-footed Beasts* (1607) 11/IV 29/VII. G. Toulouze *Livre
de Fleurs, Feuilles, et Oyzeaus* (1656) 12/V. L. Trattinnick
Ausgemahlte Tafeln (1813-14) 6/VIII. P. Treveris *The Grete
Herball* (1526) 9/VIII. E. Twining *The Chief Natural Orders
of Plants* (1849) 21/V. P. Vallet *Le jardin du Roy* (1623) 3/I
4/IV 28/VI 4/XII. R. Visscher *Sinne-Popper* (1614) 16/IV.
G. Whitney *A Choice of Emblemes* (1586) 29/VIII.
H. Wilson *The Chronicles of a Garden* (1864) 18/VIII.
G. Wither *A Collection of Emblemes* (1635) 1/II 28/IV 4/V
19/VIII 28/IX. W. Woodville *Medical Botany* (1790) 21/I.
J. Worlidge *Vinetum Britannicum* (1678) 16/X.

JANUARY

so called, after *Janus*, a pretended Deity, who the
Romans supposed presided over the Beginning of all
Business, and so the Year. Temperature: 38.4°
Fahrenheit (3.6° Celsius). Rainfall: 1.89 inches (5 cm).

1

Laurustinus, *Viburnum tinus*

A frosty January will befriend you more than a mild November.

'I have often wondered that those who are like my self, and love to live in Gardens, have never thought of contriving a Winter Garden, which should consist of such Trees only as never cast their Leaves. We have very often little Snatches of Sunshine, and Fair Weather, in the most uncomfortable Parts of the Year, and have frequently several Days in November and January, that are as agreeable as any in the finest months. At such times, therefore, I think there could not be a greater Pleasure, than to walk in such a Winter Garden as I have proposed.'
Joseph Addison *The Spectator* 6 September 1712

2

Groundsel, *Senecio vulgaris*

The seed catalogues are published in the winter and should be asked for by those not on the seedsmen's books, and lists should be made out as soon as they arrive, the first week in January if possible.

'In our variable climate, what is to be done this month, depends much on the state of the weather; but, if it is not deep snow, there is always something to be done advantageously. Even deep snow gives time for cleaning, thrashing, and sorting seeds, preparing stakes and pea-sticks, tying mats, sorting bulbs, and many similar sorts of employment. Dry frost makes an opportunity of manuring land with ease and neatness, and also pruning gooseberries, currants, and other hardy shrubs, and of clearing away dead trees and bushes, and thinning others. Turn dunghills and compost heaps. I say it at once for the whole year, destroy vermin wherever you can find them.'
William Cobbett *The English Gardener* 1829

Persian Iris, *Iris persica*

Work out a cropping scheme for the vegetable garden. Marsh titmouse commences to sing.

'The earliest iris to bloom, the bulbous *Iris persica*, tiny, impetuous, and fragrant, with its green, violet, and gold blossom pushing out of the soil in March and April, is hardy in our eastern gardens, as is the better-known *Iris reticulata*. The foliage of these bulbous irises disappears in the summer, so their positions must be carefully marked.'
Ella Porter McKinney, New Jersey 1927 (*Our Garden Heritage* ed. Alice Sloane Anderson 1961)

3

Hazel, *Corylus avellana*

Complete as soon as possible the digging of vacant ground. Hen chaffinches flock together.

   'Kate, like the hazel twig
So straight and slender, and as brown in hue
As hazel-nuts and sweeter than the kernels.'
William Shakespeare *The Taming of the Shrew* 1596

4

5

Hellebore, *Helleborus foetidus*

Winter aconite in bloom

'To destroy Moles. Take some white or black hellebore, the white of an egg, some wheat flower, milk, and a little sweet wine, or mead; make it up into a paste, and put pellets of the size of a nut into their holes, which being greedily eaten by them, will occasion their death. Put two or three heads of garlick, leeks, or onions, into their holes, and they will run out greatly terrified, so that they may then be easily caught by means of a dog.'
William Thompson *The New Gardener's Calendar* 1779

6

Screw Moss, *Tortula rigida*

As the days lengthen, the frosts strengthen. White dead nettle flowering.

'This month is commonly frosty, and if we have any great Snow in the Course of the whole Year, it is about this Time. In this Month the *Thames* has been three times frozen within the Space of forty Years; and it is observable, that the most piercing Cold reigns chiefly at this Season: Therefore what is nice and curious in our Gardens, must now be diligently look'd after, especially those Plants which are in Hot-Beds, by taking proper Means to defend them from the cold Air, and covering the Glasses a little before Sun-set with Litter and Mats.'
Richard Bradley *The Gentleman and Gardeners Kalendar* 1718

Portugal Laurel, *Prunus lusitanica*

7

Now is the proper season to construct a summer-house in a garden. Robin commences to sing.

'The mere fact of the variability of the seasons should be sufficient to convince the most doubting that what may be right one year may be wrong next. If a calendar of garden events is kept it will be readily seen by reference what a difference there can be in the annual happenings.'
Harry Pierce and Alec Mawson *Shrubs* 1935

'The winter Aconites will give my first mass of colour in the New Year. I like a garden which has always some brilliant display in evidence, as well as containing interesting and beautiful single plants.'
Harry Roberts *The Chronicle of a Cornish Garden* 1901

Yellow Tremella, *Tremella deliquescens*

8

Coconut fibre is a useful substance among flowering plants at this season. Mistle thrush sings.

'Here it may be well to remark, that many people who neglect to provide themselves with pea-rods at this season, when it can be so conveniently done, are necessitated, when the hurry of business overtakes them in spring, to sow their peas and let them trail on the ground; in which situation they will never produce, especially the tall growing kinds, one third as many as if they were properly rodded.'
Bernard MacMahon *The American Gardener's Calendar* 1806

9

Common Laurel, *Prunus lauro-cerasus*

Tomato seeds may now be sown in a temperature of about 70°, so as to secure early plants for indoor culture.

'But let the months go round, a few short months,
And all shall be restor'd. These naked shoots,
Barren as lances, among which the wind
Makes wintry music, sighing as it goes,
Shall put their graceful foliage on again,
And, more aspiring, and with ampler spread,
Shall boast new charms, and more than they
        have lost.'
William Cowper *The Task* 1785

10

Gorse, *Ulex Europaeus*

Fork over the ground in the shrub garden and remove any suckers from rhododendrons, lilacs and similar subjects.

'The season most trying to those who are interested in the operations of gardening is rapidly passing away, and the amateur may begin to take heart, and expect that his labours will soon be crowned with success. It is true, we are not yet in the middle of January, and that the proverb may prove correct, "As the day lengthens the cold strengthens"; still a large portion of the dullest and worst weather is gone, and the development of early spring will soon be visible. Since the beginning of October, the gardener has stood on the defensive, awaiting and dreading the combined attacks of damp and frost, and comparative darkness; but now three months of this state of anxiety have passed away, and even if there were no other circumstances of a cheerful character than the departure of this long period of watching, this would be something.'
Henry Burgess *The Amateur Gardener* 1854

Early Moss, *Bryum hornum*

11

**Common bunting commences to sing.
This month prepare dung for your garden;
and the dung of pigeons or poultry is excellent
for asparagus and strawberries, when it has
passed the first heat.**

'When this month proves frosty, so as the
ground is frozen so hard as not to be dug (as it
often happens) then you may carry dung upon
the Ground, repair hedges, rub out and clean
your seeds, and prepare all your tools ready for
use against the frost's going off, that you may
not be hindered with these things when every
other part of the business is in great haste.'
Philip Miller *The Gardeners Kalendar* 1732

Hygrometic Moss, *Funaria hygrometica*

12

**The herb bed should be put as near the house
as possible, that unnecessary trampling on the
paths may be avoided in bad weather.**

'The mosses put forth their singular and minute
parts of fructification during the Winter months;
and offer a most curious spectacle to the
botanist, at a time when all the rest of Nature is
dead to him.'
The Book of Months 1844

'The Herbaceous Border voices all too plainly
the month of Death, which the old Gaelic rann
associates with January. A careful search,
however, among the withered leaves of the
past year reveals one or two brave hepaticas
showing colour.'
Lucy H. Soutar *Monthly Gleanings in a Scottish Garden*
1909

13

Common Yew Tree, *Taxus baccata*

The gardener, during this month, does not labour in the garden more than five hours a day, allowing one hour more for early and late attendance on hot-house fires, and seven for sleep, there remains eleven hours for personal improvement.

'Yew trees live to a great age, the timber is hard ("a post of yew outlives a post of iron"), the leaves are poisonous, and the berries are red. So the Yew was a protective, offensively defensive tree, one of the best to plant by your house, and the very best (though other timbers were as elastic) to make into bows. The Yew beside the house, near to the gables and the chimneys, not only protected but looked comforting. It tied the house to the landscape.'
Geoffrey Grigson *The Englishman's Flora* 1955

14

Barren Strawberry, *Fragaria sterilis*

Either the coldest or the wettest day in the year. Hedge accentor commences to sing.

'Strawberries grew wild for the most part, but may have been brought into cultivation here and there because they improve so much as a result. They were popular in Anglo-Saxon times; the Countess of Leicester bought some for her household in 1265; the trend-setting Earl of Lincoln may have grown them in his Holborn garden; in 1328 Edward III's accountant recorded the purchase of "one silver fork of strawberries"; by the fifteenth century they were so fashionable that they may have been cultivated more than the record suggests.... They were sweet and colourful...and were one of the increasing number of fruits cultivated by the prosperous bourgeoisie in the fifteenth century.'
Teresa McLean *Medieval English Gardens* 1981

Ivy, *Hedera helix*

15

The slug makes its appearance and commences its depredation on garden plants and green wheat.

'The greater Ivie climbeth on trees, old buildings, and walls: the stalkes thereof are wooddy, and now and then so great as it seems to become a tree; from which it sendeth forth a multitude of little boughes or branches every way, whereby as it were with armes it creepeth and wandereth far about: it also bringeth forth continually fine roots, by which it fastneth it selfe and cleaveth wonderfull hard upon trees, and upon the smoothest walls: the leaves are smooth, shining on the upper side, cornered with sharpe pointed corners. The floures are very small and mossie, after which succeed bundles of black berries, every one having a small sharped pointall. The leaves laid in steepe in water for a day and a nights space, helpe sore and smarting waterish eies, if they be bathed and washed with the water wherein they have beene infused.'
John Gerard *Herball* 1597

Common Red Dead Nettle, *Lamium purpureum*

16

An alpine house is the richest joy of January. Before the end of January the seed beds must be worked into a good state of cultivation for seed sowing.

'Hard frost. The market gardeners felt the severity of the weather – it stopped their labours, and some of the men, attended by their wives, went about in parties, and with frosted greens fixed at the top of rakes and hoes, uttered the ancient cry of "Pray remember the gardeners! Remember the poor frozen out gardeners!" '
Morning Herald 16 January 1826

17

Garden Anemone, *Anemone hortensis*

Earth worms lie out on the ground and the snail appears.

'Forsaken. This flower derives its name from *anemos*, the Greek word for wind, from thence came our poetical appellation of "the wind-flower". The ancients tells us that Anemone was formerly a nymph beloved by Zephyr, and that Flora, jealous of her beauty, banished her from her Court, and finally transformed her into the flower that now bears her name. The more common myth is, that the anemone sprang from the blood of Adonis, combined with the tears which Venus shed over his body.'
The Language of Flowers 19th century

18

Four-toothed Moss, *Bryum pellucidum*

Hedges of beech, hornbeam, quick, privet and plum may be clipped now.

'Against mickle cold; take nettles, seethe them in oil, smear and rub all thine body therewith: the cold will depart away.'
Leech Book of Bald 10th Century

'Why grass is green, or why our blood is red,
Are mysteries which none have reached unto.'
John Donne 1573–1631 *Human Ignorance*

White Dead Nettle, *Lamium album*

**Design the flower border. Song thrush
commences to sing.**

19

'The Dead Nettle or Archangell. They flower
from the beginning of the spring, all the Sommer
long. The flowers of the white Archangells are
preserved or conserved daily to be used, or the
distilled water of them is used to stay the whites,
and those of the red to stay the reds in women,
and is thought good to make the heart merry, to
drive away melancholy, and to quicken the
spirits.'
John Parkinson *Theatrum Botanicum* 1640

Woolly Dead Nettle, *Lamium garganicum*

**Even in the most sterile months of winter
a neat garden possesses attractions, while
a slovenly one, however extensive and well
filled, seems to combine with the asperities
of the season in rendering itself hideous.**

20

'Most pitiless and stark the winter grew
Meanwhile beneath a sky of cloudless blue,
And sun that warmed not, till they nigh forgot
The green lush spring, the summer rich and hot,
The autumn fragrant with slow-ripening fruit.'
William Morris *The Life and Death of Jason* 1867

21

Black Hellebore, *Helleborus niger*

**Aquarius: 21 January–19 February.
Great titmouse begins to sing.**

'There are several kinds of Hellebore, but the two varieties usually seen in English gardens are more familiar under their prettier names of Christmas rose and Lenten rose, Helleborus niger and Helleborus orientalis respectively. Why the Christmas rose, which is white, should be called black in Latin I could not imagine until I discovered that the adjective referred to the root; but I still cannot imagine why people do not grow both these varieties more freely. They will fill up many an odd corner; their demands are few; and they will give flowers at a time of year when flowers are scarce.'
Vita Sackville-West *In Your Garden* 1951

22

Early Whitlow Grass, *Draba verna*

Francis Bacon born in 1561 in London; scientist and essayist; made a garden at Gray's Inn.

'I do hold it in the royal ordering of Gardens, there ought to be Gardens for all the months in the year, in which, severally, things of beauty may be then in season.'
Francis Bacon *Of Gardens* 1625

'The tools it is impossible to do without are the fork, spade, hoe and rake, and the same can really be said of garden shears and secateurs, the first for grass and hedge cutting and the second for pruning. Small hand trowels and forks are invaluable for the more fiddly jobs.'
Percy Thrower *In Your Garden* 1959

Peziza, *Peziza acetabulum*

23

Repair storm damage. Plant quickset hedges. On 23 January 1971 a record US low of minus 78° Fahrenheit was recorded in Prospect Creek, Alaska. Skylarks begin to sing.

'Bullfinches and Tits do considerable harm to Currant and Gooseberry trees by destroying the buds; this harm is best combated by twisting black cotton in and out among the branches, rather than by killing these songsters and damaging the trees with shot.'
Geoffrey Henslow *The Gardener's Calendar* 1925

Stalkless Moss, *Phascum muticum*

24

Mend and repair all your decayed espaliers with new poles, where they want them, and fasten such places where the poles or rails are loose with wire, which is the strongest fastening.

'Moss. Maternal Love. J. J. Rousseau, so long tormented by his own passions, and persecuted by those of others, consoled and embellished the evening of his days by botanical researches. Above all, the study of mosses delighted him. It is they, he often said, which confer youth and freshness on our plains; embellishing nature at the moment that the flowers disappear. On the confines of the world, the Laplanders cover their subterraneous dwellings with moss; and then collecting their families round them they defy the prolonged period of their half-year's winter. Their numerous herds of reindeer know no other nourishment than the moss: and the female Laplanders form cradles of the same warm and verdant materials for their offspring.'
The Language of Flowers 1834

25

Winter Hellebore, *Helleborus hyemalis*

St Paul's Day. Rooks resort to their nesting trees.

'If St Paul's Day be faire and cleare,
It doth forebode a fruitfull yeare.'
Old saying

'On this day prognostications of the months were drawn for the whole year. If fair, and clear, there was to be plenty; if cloudy, or misty, much cattle would die; if rain, or snow fell, then it presaged a dearth; and if windy, there would be wars.'
Mrs E. W. Wirt *Flora's Dictionary* 1855

26

White Butterbur, *Tussilago albu*

Now is the time, after a shower, to cleanse fruit trees of moss, their great enemy.

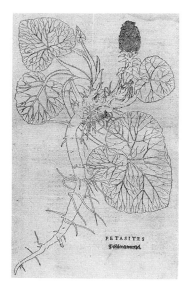

'Collecting manures. This is a general sort of duty in the winter months. Peat earth, road-drift, dead leaves and vegetable matter, sand, marl, loam, turves for rotting in heaps, horse, cow, sheep's, poultry, and pig's dung, and all other stuffs useful in composts, should be gathered together, but always in separate heaps, to lie until wanted. Leaves take two years to rot, and sometimes more; turves will be over three, although usable at the end of two.'
George Glenny *Hand-Book to the Flower Garden and Greenhouse* 1873

Earth Moss, *Phascum cuspidatum*

27

Turn over pretty often your heaps of compost, that the frost may mellow them, and break the clods. In mild weather, make new heaps of compost, because they should have time to lie and sweeten before they are used.

'This moneth is the rich mans charge, and the poor mans misery; the cold like the days increase, yet qualified with the hopes and expectations of the approaching Spring: The Trees, Meadows and Fields are now naked, unless cloathed in white, whilest the Countryman sits at home, and enjoys the fruit of his past labour, and contemplates on his intended Enterprises. Now is welcom a cup of good Cider, or other excellent Liquors, such that you prepared the Autumn before; moderately taken, it proves the best Physic.'
John Worlidge *Kalendarium Rusticum* 1675

Double Daisy, *Bellis perennis plenus*

28

A single snowdrop or two in the garden, and perhaps here and there a primrose on a bank, come out about this time in mild seasons.

'Bellis. This innocent flower, this toy of lovers and children, derives its Latin name from the word meaning "War", because of its supposed value on the battlefield to staunch the wounds of the fallen; and "to lie beneath the daisies" has become the synonym for death. (Keats said that he felt the daisies growing over him, not long before he died.) It was also supposed to have the power of stunting growth; the juice "given to little dogs with milke, keepeth them from growing great".'
Alice Coats *Flowers and Their Histories* 1956

29

Flowering Fern, *Osmunda regalis*

If you have Iris stylosa planted in the garden, you may begin to look for the first buds; even in January it will throw up a few in favourable years.

'We are calling the gardens of the homeless transitory in an effort to define them as a type of garden. But our definition has within itself a certain inaccuracy. The truth is that all gardens are *transitory* – more like our lives, less like architecture: we build them to give an illusion of permanence. In this way too they resemble our lives.'
Diana Balmori and Margaret Morton *Transitory Gardens, Uprooted Lives* 1993

30

Spleenwort, *Asplenium trichomanes*

Priscilla Wakefield born in 1751 in Tottenham, London; author of natural history books for children.

'May it [botany] become a substitute for some of the trifling, not to say pernicious, objects, that too frequently occupy the leisure of young ladies of fashionable manners, and, by employing their faculties rationally, act as an antidote to levity and idleness.'
Priscilla Wakefield *An Introduction to Botany, in a Series of Familiar Letters* 1796

'Lawns, it seems to me, are against nature, barren and often threadbare – the enemy of a good garden. For the same trouble as mowing, you could have a year's vegetables: runner beans, cauliflowers and cabbages, mixed with pinks and peonies, shirley poppies and delphiniums.'
Derek Jarman *Derek Jarman's Garden* 1995

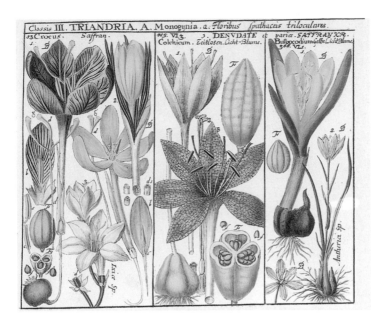

Hart's Tongue, *Asplenium scolopendrium*

Winter hellebore or aconite flowers, in mild weather, at or even before this time, and continues to blow through February.

'There followeth, for the latter part of January and February, the Mezereon-tree, which then blossoms: Crocus Vernus, both the yellow and the gray; Primroses, Anemones, the early Tulip, the Hyacinthus Orientalis, Chamairis Fritellaria.'
Francis Bacon *Of Gardens* 1625

'In the apparently dull months of winter, we have all the pleasures which expectation and the conception of infinite possibilities can give.'
Harry Roberts *The Chronicle of a Cornish Garden* 1901

31

FEBRUARY

takes its Name from *Februare,* to make expiatory
Sacrifices. It was this Month the Romans made
Sacrifices to the dead. Temperature: 39.5° Fahrenheit
(4.2° Celsius). Rainfall: 1.57 inches (4 cm).

Bay Tree, *Laurus nobilis*

1

Bees. The fittest time to establish an apiary is early in the year, about the month of February.

'In this year 1399 in a manner throughout all the realm of England, old bay trees withered, and contrary to all men's thinking grew green again, a strange sight, and supposed to import some unknown event.'
Holinshed Chronicles 1577

'This Moneth is usually subject to much Rain or Snow: if it prove either, it is not to be accounted unseasonable; the Proverb being, February fill Dike, with either black or white.'
John Worlidge *Kalendarium Rusticum* 1675

Snowdrop, *Galanthus nivalis*

2

Candlemas. Sunshine on this day is a bad omen. Early in February shallots may be planted.

'If Candlemas-day be fair and bright,
Winter will have another flight.
But if Candlemas-day be clouds and rain,
Winter is gone, and will not come again.'
Old Almanack

3

Great Water Moss, *Fontinalis antipyretica*

Moles go to work in throwing up their hillocks as soon as the earth is softened. Spurge laurel flowering.

'Take red Herrings, and cutting them in pieces, burn the pieces on the Mole-hills; or you may put Garlic or Leeks in the Mouths of their Hills, and the Moles will leave the ground. I have not tryed these ways, and therefore refer the Reader to his own tryal, belief, or doubt.'
Robert Sharrock *The History of the Propagation and Improvement of Vegetables* 1660

'The worst Enemyes to gardens are Moles, Catts, Earewiggs, Snailes and Mice, and they must bee carefully destroyed, or all your labor all the year long is lost. The only assur'd meanes to destroy moles is by watching them heave at sun rising and setting, and then casting them forth with a spade, or striking them with a Mole speare.'
Thomas Hanmer *The Garden Book* 1659

4

Common Hair Moss or Goldilocks, *Polytrichum commune*

Double daisies begin in mild seasons to blow and ornament cottage gardens about this time.

'When October and November are warm and rainy, January and February are frosty and cold: but if October and November be snow and frost, then January and February are open and mild. If the sun rises red and fiery, it certainly betokens more or less wind and rain. This observation agrees with the old English rule:
    If red the sun begins his race,
    Be sure that rain will fall apace.'
Samuel Cooke *The Complete English Gardener* 1780

Common Primrose, *Primula vulgaris*

5

Winter jasmine will flower on walls of any aspect, it layers easily, and the layers can be taken off in February and planted where they are wanted.

'Of all the Primula family none excel our native Primroses in loveliness, and they are the earliest of all to flower. Some of the prettiest of the wild varieties are worthy of being introduced into shrubberies and semi-wild places. All the varieties are readily increased by division of the offsets, or by seeds, which are produced in abundance. Shelter and partial shade are the conditions chiefly necessary to their successful culture.'
William Robinson *The English Flower Garden* 1883

Blue Hyacinth, *Hyacinthus orientalis*

6

Catkins of the willow appear. Hazels in flower. If the weather allows, buddleias, dogwood and vines must all be pruned in February.

'Sorrowful. I am sorry. According to the mythologists, this fairy-like fragile flower had its origin in the death of Hyacinthus, a Spartan youth, greatly favoured by Apollo. He fell a victim to the jealous rage of Zephyrus, who, in revenge for the preference manifested for him by the Sun-god, had determined to effect his destruction. Accordingly, one day when Hyacinthus was playing at quoits with his divine friend, Zephyrus blew so powerfully upon the quoit flung by Apollo that it struck the unfortunate prince on the temple and killed him, to the intense grief of his innocent slayer. To commemorate the grace and beauty of the dead youth, Apollo, unable to restore him to life, caused the flower which now bears his name to spring from his blood.'
The Language of Flowers 19th Century

P.J. Redouté pinx.

7

Round-leafed Cyclamen, *Cyclamen coum*

Blanche Elizabeth Edith Henrey born in 1906 in Brentford, Middlesex; gardening bibliographer.

'It was originally planned that the period covered by the present undertaking should be from the earliest times until 1850. The final date, however, was changed to 1800 when it was found that more than twice as many works were published during the first fifty years of the nineteenth century as during the years previous to 1800.'
Blanche Henrey *British Botanical and Horticultural Literature before 1800* 1975

8

Narrow-leafed Moss, *Mnium androgynum*

If depressions have formed on your lawn, now is the time to repair the damage by lifting the turf and putting down good sifted soil.

'There are delicate pleasures ahead known only to us country-dwellers. The smell of wild cherry bark in the woods, that fugitive delicious fragrance which we may catch only in early February on soft damp days, the first signal that the sap-tide is on the upward flow; and presently the scent of the plumed larches, and the daphnes again in bloom.'
Marion Cran 1875-1942 *Private Papers (Bedside Marion Cran)*1951

Roman Narcissus, *Narcissus romanus*

9

Henry Arthur Bright born in 1830 in Liverpool; partner in shipping firm and gardening writer.

'In front of one of the beds of evergreens on the lawn I planted some double Primroses – yellow, white, red, and lilac; some of them are showing their blossoms, but they are not vigorous. By the way, I found it very difficult to get these Primroses, and had to pay what seemed an excessive price for them. They are, I fear, among the old neglected flowers, which we run a good chance of losing altogether, if gardeners will confine themselves entirely to bedding plants.'
Henry Arthur Bright *A Year in a Lancashire Garden* 1879

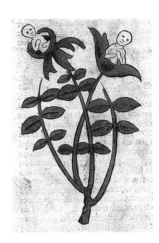

Mezereon, *Daphne mezereon*

10

Bullfinches return to our gardens in February and, though timid half the year, are now fearless and persevering.

'*Chimomanthus fragrans*, in English the Winter-sweet, should have a place of honour. Although it was introduced from China so long ago as 1766, it is not often seen now except in the older gardens, and in honesty I should warn purchasers of young plants that it will not begin to flower until it is five or six years old. But it is worth waiting for. Extremely sweet-scented, even in the cold open air, long sprigs loaded with the strange maroon-and-yellow flowers can be cut all through January and February; it lasts for two or three weeks in water, especially if you smash the stems with a hammer, a hint which applies to all hard-wooded growth.'
Vita Sackville-West *In Your Garden* 1951

11

Red Primrose, *Primula vern-rubra*

Early salads should receive much attention from the gardener this month and regular sowings should be made of mustard, cress and radish.

'You must now dig and prepare your ground for Carrots, Onions, Leeks, Radishes, Spinach, and Cabbage-Lettuce, which should now be sown; but where it is only for the supply of a family, there should not be too much of each sort sown at once; For it is a much better way to sow three or four times of each sort at about ten days distance from each other, that there may be a continuation of them for the kitchen, than to trust to one sowing, which will last but a short time: Besides, if the first or second sowing should miscarry, it is probable the other may do well, and then there will be no disappointment of a crop.'
Philip Miller *The Gardeners Kalendar* 1732

12

Anemone, *Anemone hepatica*

Heartsease or pansy flowers in mild seasons. Green woodpeckers call.

'The Anemones likewise or Windeflowers are so full of variety and so dainty, so pleasant and so delightsome flowers, that the sight of them doth enforce an earnest longing desire in the minde of any one to be a possessour of some of them at the least: For without all doubt, this one kinde of flower, so variable in colours, so differing in forme (being almost as many sorts of them double as single) so plentifull in bearing flowers, and so durable in lasting, and also so easie both to preserve and encrease, is of it selfe alone almost sufficient to furnish a garden with their flowers for almost halfe the yeare.'
John Parkinson *Paradisus* 1629

Polyanthus, *Primula polyantha*

John Reid born in 1656 in Niddry Castle near Edinburgh; gardener and author of the first book for gardeners published in Scotland.

13

'The Gard'ners year is a circle as their labour, never at an end.'
John Reid *The Scots Gard'ner* 1683

'Failures and absurdities are of course abundant in the beginning of our experimental career, but what should we do without them?'
Dean Hole *Our Gardens* 1899

Yellow Crocus, *Crocus moesiacus*, or *Crocus aureus*

St Valentine's Day. Any pruning that has been put off should be done this month. Common speedwell in flower.

14

'Kew has been marked out by the suffragettes as one of the scenes of their exploits. They smashed a quantity of glass in the orchid house, and, in a manner that one can scarcely accredit to sane adults, wantonly tried to destroy the plants. Rare and delicate plants, under bell-glasses, attracted the special venom of these feminists.'
Journal of Horticulture and Home Farmer 1913

15

Cloth of Gold Crocus, *Crocus sulphureus*

Broad beans can be sown in the open ground in mild weather in February. Coltsfoot flowers.

'I wonder if the sap is stirring yet,
If wintry birds are dreaming of a mate,
If frozen snowdrops feel as yet the sun
And crocus fires are kindling one by one:
Sing, robin, sing;
I still am sore in doubt concerning Spring.'
Christina Rossetti 1830–94 *The First Spring Day*

16

Lilac Primrose, *Primula acaulis plena*

Persian iris flowers, but requires shelter. Yellowhammer utters its characteristic notes. Coppice woodland for fuel.

'I was a very small boy when I first essayed to grow Primulas and Auriculas in the garden of my old home in Angus. Then, and since, I received the utmost encouragement and much valuable advice from my father, always a keen gardener, and it was from him that I got my first plants.'
Kenneth Corsar *Primulas in the Garden* 1948

Scotch Crocus, *Crocus susianus*

Reginald John Farrer born in 1880 in Clapham, Yorkshire; plant collector and gardening writer who influenced the development of rock-gardening.

'It has been my endeavour, all through the book indeed, to preserve the vivid and personal note, at any cost to the arid grey gravity usually considered necessary to the dignity of a dictionary.'
Reginald Farrer *The English Rock-Garden* 1919

17

Wall Speedwell, *Veronica vernus arvensis*

Rev Henry Nicholson Ellacombe born in 1822 in Bitton, Gloucestershire; Rector of Bitton in 1850, where he made a garden and wrote about gardening.

18

'Of all February flowers I suppose the snowdrop is the most popular. Its thorough hardiness, its patience under any ill-treatment, its easy cultivation, and, above all, its pure beauty, make it welcome to every garden, and there is no more valued plant in the garden of the poor, and in children's gardens. The common name is not the old name, and certainly, to nearly the end of the seventeenth century, it was described as the white bulbous violet. I suppose snowdrop was adopted from the common names of the flower in its native countries, such as France and Germany. Its German names may be translated as snowflake, February flower, naked maiden, snow-violet, and snowdrop; and its French names as the white bell, the bell of the snows, the bell of winter, and the snow-piercer.'
Canon Ellacombe *In a Gloucestershire Garden* 1895

19

Field Speedwell, *Veronica agrestis*

The first bird's nest in spring. Mice are very destructive to gardens about this season, as they attack the corms of the crocuses and other similar plants.

'Bring orchis, bring the foxglove spire,
The little speedwell's darling blue,
Deep tulips dash'd with fiery dew,
Laburnums, dropping-wells of fire.'
Alfred Tennyson *In Memoriam* 1850

20

Hound's Tongue, *Cynoglossum omphalodes* or *C. lusitanicum*

Pisces: 20 February–20 March. February is a good month to propagate chrysanthemum cuttings.

On 20 February 1913 at 3 a.m. the Refreshment Pavilion at Kew was seen to be on fire. A week later *The Journal of Horticulture and Home Farmer* reported with outrage: 'For the second time within a fortnight female vandals have visited Kew Gardens with direful consequences. The picturesque tea pavilion was razed to the ground by fire. Happily the perpetrators were captured and are unlikely to resume their insane campaign for some time to come.'

White Crocus, *Crocus albus*

Destroy snails and other vermin; if they escape this month, they will make great havoc. Common nettle in flower.

'The great white *Crocus*, rising up With narrow long green leaves with a white line in the middle of them; from these cometh up, cover'd with a white skin, small low white flowers, of six leaves, a long saffron pointel in the middle, with some Chives about it: Not opening but when the Sun shines.'
Samuel Gilbert *The Gardener's Almanack* 1683

21

Herb Margaret, *Bellis perennis*

Daisy or herb Margaret is now seen in the meadows and opens its pleasing flowers here and there in warm days: in the evening daisies close their flowers.

22

'Pigs are paying animals if you have a good kitchen garden and some wash from the house to give them, and their manure is very precious. Straw should be given them for their bed, and this makes a valuable addition to your soil. The usual plan is to buy two young pigs early in the year and sell them in the Autumn. Pigs should never be given any meat scraps, tea leaves, or coffee grounds; they will eat anything in the way of vegetables.'
Mrs Earle and Ethel Case *Gardening for the Ignorant* 1912

23

Apricot Tree, *Prunus armeniaca*

Agnes Arber born in 1879 in London; lecturer in botany at University College, London; authority on herbals.

'The present writer was once told by a man who was born in 1842 that, during his boyhood in Bedfordshire, he was acquainted with a cottager who treated the ailments of her neighbours with the help of a copy of Gerard's *Herball*. If, as is most likely, this was one of Johnson's editions, she must thence have known certain illustrations copied from Anicia Juliana's manuscript of Dioscorides made soon after AD 500 – figures which were probably themselves derived from the work of Krateuas, belonging to the century before Christ. We thus catch a glimpse of the herbal tradition passing unbroken through two thousand years, from Krateuas, the Greek, to an old woman poring over her well thumbed picture book in an English village.'
Agnes Arber *Herbals* 1912

24

Great Fern, *Osmunda regalis*

The onion bed should be got ready in February. There is no need to have fresh ground for onions every year, as they do well for a number of years in the same place.

'Though ferns are beautiful anywhere, and may suitably adorn the trim border, and mingle with ornaments of formal design, they are more at home, more befitting among tree-stumps, and in boldly designed rock-work, or water-scenery, where they appear in their proper character of wildness and simplicity.'
Shirley Hibberd *Rustic Adornments for Homes of Taste* 1856

Peach-blossom, *Amigdalus persica*

25

A well-made walk ought to be dry enough for walking on five minutes after the termination of a twelve hours' rain.

'There is no flowering Shrub excells, if equals, that of a Peach or Apple-tree in Bloom. The tender enammell'd Blossoms, verdant Foliage, with such a glorious Embroidery of Festoons and Fruitages, wafting their Odours on every Blast of Wind; And at last bowing down their laden Branches, ready to yield their pregnant offspring into the Hands of their laborious Planter and Owner.'
Stephen Switzer *The Practical Fruit-Gardener* 1724

Lesser Periwinkle, *Vinca minor*

26

The end of February is the right time for dressing lawns and grass paths. If they are mossy, they are best well raked; if weedy, the weeds must be removed with a spud or old knife.

'Tender Recollections. In France the Periwinkle, which there is sometimes called "the magician's violet", is considered the emblem of sincere friendship, and as such is much used in their language of flowers. The English have adopted this evergreen plant as the representative of *tender recollections*. In Italy the country people make garlands of this plant, to place upon the biers of their deceased children, for which reason they name it the "flower of death". But in Germany it is the symbol of *immortality*; and, because its fine glossy myrtle-green leaves flourish all through the winter, they term it "winter verdure".'
The Language of Flowers 19th Century

27

Lungwort, *Pulmonaria officinalis*

Now is the time the bullfinch doth the greatest harm to the buds of fruit trees. Rocket should be sown in a warm border in February, and during the next months if a succession is wanted.

'Potatoes are not known in the South parts of England, yet in the North parts they are planted in poor and rich mens Gardens, for the goodness that they yeeld to their tables in the winter when no other roots are to be had; in Ireland they are so generall and so common, that I never saw any man that had land and habitation there but that he had store of Potatoes for his use.'
Stephen Blake *The Compleat Gardeners Practice* 1664

28

Purple Crocus, *Crocus vernus*

By the end of the month a first sowing of all the best annuals may be made for planting out in the borders. Vipers begin to appear.

'Cheerfulness. Hope. According to some authors, these bright little flowers derive their name from a Greek word signifying thread, from the fact of their *thread* or filament being in such request for saffron dye. The Greeks fabled that Crocu, a beautiful youth, was transformed into this flower; as his lady-love, Smilax, was at the same time into a yew-tree. It is in England consecrated to St Valentine.'
The Language of Flowers 19th Century

Purple Crocus, *Crocus vernus*

In light warm soils, the first potatoes may be planted at the end of February.

'In Leap Year, it is a common notion that broad Beans grow the wrong way, i.e., the seed is set in the pods in quite the contrary way to what it is in other years. The reason given is that, because it is the ladies' year, the Beans always lie the wrong way – in reference to the privilege possessed by the fair sex of courting in Leap Year.'
Richard Folkard *Plants and Lore, Legends, and Lyrics* 1884

MARCH

was named after the God *Mars*, by Romulus,
and is the first Month of the Roman Martial Year.
Temperature: 41.8° Fahrenheit (5.6° Celsius).
Rainfall: 1.55 inches (4 cm).

Common Leek, *Allium porrum*

1

St David's Day. Leek worn today by the Welsh. Rooks building their nests. The ivy-leafed speedwell flowers. March comes in like a lion and goes out like a lamb.

'March is a month of promises – some kept, some thrown into the discard. To the owner of a garden it seems to me the most exciting and provocative month of the year. March holds careless traffic with blizzards, with caressing zephyrs, with gray, downpouring rains, with suns warm as May's, with frivolous snow flurries, tender spring showers, thunder and lightning, fierce cold and what have you. One's aroused enthusiasm goes up and down with the eccentricities of the thermometer and the barometer, and one is alternately lured forth to prowl among the beds and borders and thrust back rudely to the glowing hearth and the solace of books and catologs.'
Louise Beebe Wilder *Adventures in a Suburban Garden* 1931

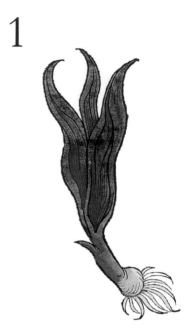

Dwarf Mouse-ear Chickweed, *Cerastium pumilum*

2

Geoffrey Edward Harvey Grigson born in 1905 in Pelynt, Cornwall; writer and broadcaster.

'I suspect that a fifteenth-century or fourteenth-century housewife knew many more wild and cultivated plants than most country housewives know today. She had to; and the magic mixed with her botanical knowledge and medicinal knowledge was not surprising. After all, how remarkable that if you eat a plant, it keeps you alive! How remarkable that some plants do the opposite, and do it with dispatch; that others affect the mind narcotically and strangely; that others have local effects on your body inside and out!'
Geoffrey Grigson *The Englishman's Flora* 1955

3

Golden-fig Marigold, *Mesembryanthemum aureum*

This day is called Pruniflora in the Latin calendar because the beautiful white blossoms of the early plum are already expanded.

'With the first mild day that comes in March the thoughts of all garden lovers, who spend the winter months in the round of city life, fly away to their gardens.'
Helena Rutherfurd Ely *Another Hardy Garden Book* 1905

'Yellow-gold is the colour of the month. Daffodil, coltsfoot, aconite, marsh marigold, buttercup, and dandelion are all of the same hue.'
William Beach Thomas *An Observer's Twelvemonth* 1923

4

Common Chickweed, *Alsine media*

This well known weed is now in flower and so continues all the spring. Chickweed is gathered in vast quantities about London for various song birds, who are kept in cages in town, and who are very fond of it, as well as groundsel.

'Make ready a plot
for seedes for the pot.
For garden best,
is south southwest.'
Thomas Tusser *Five Hundreth Points of Good Husbandry* 1573

'Dogs & cats applyed to the rootes of trees before the sap rise, have recovered many olde decaying trees. Shred them.'
Hugh Platt *Floraes Paradise* 1608

Green Hellebore, *Helleborus viridis*

Stake and bind up your weakest herbs or plants against the violence of winds that usually happen this month. Willows in bloom.

5

'Blackthorn. This tree usually blossoms while cold NE winds blow; so that the harsh rugged weather obtaining at this season is called by the country people blackthorn winter.'
Gilbert White *The Natural History of Selborne* 1768–92

'We have a tradition, or, if you will, a superstition, in this part of the world, that rooks always begin to build on the first Sunday in March. Last year my rooks were punctual to a day.'
Henry Arthur Bright *A Year in a Lancashire Garden* 1879

Lent Lily, *Pseudo-narcissus multiplex*

Spring commences on this day and lasts ninety-three days. Pick young stinging nettles to make nettle beer. The wryneck appears.

6

'For March, there come Violets, especially the single blue, which are the earliest; the yellow Daffodil, the Daisy, the Almond-tree in blossom, the Peach-tree in blossom, the Cornelian-tree in blossom, Sweet-Briar.'
Francis Bacon *Of Gardens* 1625

7

Early Daffodil, *Narcissus simplex*

The only seedlings ready to plant out will be Antirrhinums (snapdragons), which should by this time be large enough to put in any empty space in the garden.

'Daffadowndillies, have their roots parted, and set once in three or four years, or longer time. They flower timely, and after Midsummer are scarcely seen. They are more for Ornament than for use, so are Daisies.'
William Lawson *The Country House-wifes Garden* 1617

'Frances Pryor aged 10 was charged, on a warrant, with unlawfully plucking flowers in Kew Gardens on the 7th March; and Eliza Pryor, her mother, was charged with aiding and abetting, contrary to the Parks' Regulation Act.'
Richmond and Twickenham Times 28 March 1885

8

Ever-blowing Rose, *Rosa semperflorens*

Apricot tree blossoms. Peacock butterfly appears.

'Today there has come up from the country one of the spring gems of the year, a large bunch of the lilac Daphne, the old *Mezereum*. It is a small shrub, not a quick grower, and most people, especially gardeners, are afraid to cut it. But is this is done bravely at the time of flowering, I think it only grows stronger and flowers better the following year, and you get the benefit of the exceedingly fragrant blossoms.'
Mrs Earle *Pot-Pourri from a Surrey Garden* 1897

Hoop-petticoat Daffodil, *Narcissus bulbocodium*

9

Vita Sackville-West born in 1892 in Knole, Kent; poet, novelist and horticultural journalist; gardening correspondent for the *Observer* 1947–61; created a famous garden at Sissinghurst, Kent.

'I am trying to make a grey, green, and white garden. This is an experiment which I ardently hope may be successful, though I doubt it. One's best ideas seldom play up in practice to one's expectations, especially in gardening, where everything looks so well on paper and in the catalogues, but fails so lamentably in fulfilment after you have tucked your plants into the soil. Still one hopes.'
Vita Sackville-West *In Your Garden* 1951

Upright Chickweed, *Veronica triphyllos*

10

Frogs spawning. Asparagus should be planted now. Tree creeper commences its spring note.

'10 March 1775. The peach trees at Monticelli in blossom. We have had the most favorable winter ever known in the memory of man. Not more than three or four snows to cover the ground, of which two might lie about two days and the others not one.'
Thomas Jefferson *Garden Book 1766–1824*

'This is generally a busy, but by no means a genial month. March dust is said to be worth a king's ransom; but the winds that upraise it are especially rough and biting, harsh and boisterous, and especially severe upon weak and tender plants; indeed, trees, plants, and shrubs that may have borne the rigours of winter with impunity, often succumb beneath the chilling blasts of March. Therefore, if any plant, not quite hardy, has not hitherto been protected, that protection should now be afforded.'
Samuel Orchart Beeton *The Book of Garden Management* 1862

11

Cornish Heath, *Erica vagans*

There are a hundred species of heaths, and four natives in this island. In the Highlands they are used in buildings, for beds and for malt liquor.

'And in the beginnyng of March or a lytell before: is tyme for a wyfe to make her garden and to get as many good sedes and herbes as she can gette: and specially suche as be good for the potte and for to eate. And oft as nede shall require it must be wedde: for else ye wede woll over growe the herbes.'
John Fitzherbert *The Boke of Husbandrie* 1523

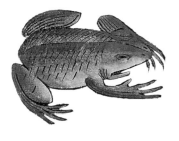

'In the wind of windy March
The catkins drop down
Curly, caterpillar-like,
Curious green and brown.'
Christina Rossetti 1828–82 *A Year's Windfalls*

12

Ixia, *Ixia bulbocodium*

Frogs are now heard croaking in the pools, ditches, ponds, and other shallow waters.

'The vegetable world begins to move and swell and the saps to rise, till in the completest silence of lone gardens and trackless plantations, where everything seems helpless and still after the bond and slavery of frost, there are bustlings, strainings, united thrusts, and pulls-all-together, in comparison with which the powerful tugs of cranes and pulleys in a noisy city are but pigmy efforts.'
Thomas Hardy *Far from the Madding Crowd* 1874

Heart's Ease, *Viola tricolor*

13

Now is a good time to divide up old iris clumps. Trim sage plants.

'Think of me. Thoughts. The *Heart's-ease*, as its French name of *pansy* or *pensée* intimates, is in the language of flowers symbolical of *remembrance*. It is a beautiful variety of the violet, far surpassing that flower in diversity and brilliancy of colour, but possessing little, if any, of the exquisite fragrance for which it is so renowned. Another of its names is "love-in-idleness", under which it has been again celebrated by Shakespeare. This tricoloured violet is also called, in various country places, "jump-up-and-kiss-me-quick"; "the herb Trinity"; "three-faces-under-a-hood"; "kiss-me-behind-the-garden-gate"; and "cuddle-me-to-you", which seems to have altered by time into the less vivacious request of "call-me-to-you".'
The Language of Flowers 19th Century

Mountain Bindweed, *Soldanella alpina*

14

Remove dead and withered leaves, and plants killed by frost. Sweetbriar comes into leaf.

'Seeds which all winter dormant lay,
Now vegetate and shoot away:
Ah, Doll! how oft thy heart has panted,
If in thy garden aught is planted!'
Poor Robin 1805

'And certainly March in our Scottish gardens is a cruel month, calling into life, with its fitful glimpses of hot sunshine, the tender shoots; then breathing upon them with its blighting breath, it seems with wanton spitefulness to play havoc among our early buds and spring flowers.'
Lucy H. Soutar *Monthly Gleanings in a Scottish Garden* 1909

15

Common Coltsfoot, *Tussilago farfara*

Liberty Hyde Bailey born in 1858 in Van Buren County, Michigan; wrote thirty-eight books on horticulture and agriculture, including *The Encyclopaedia of American Horticulture* 1900–02.

'The man who worries morning and night about the dandelions in the lawn will find great relief in loving dandelions. Each blossom is worth more than a gold coin, as it shimmers in the exuberant sunlight of the growing spring, and attracts the bees to its bosom. Little children love the dandelions: why may not we? Love the things nearest at hand; and love intensely. If I were to write a motto over the gate of a garden, I should choose the remark which Socrates made as he saw the luxuries in the market, "How much there is in the world that I do not want!" '
Liberty Hyde Bailey *Garden-Making* 1898

16

Nodding Daffodil, *Narcissus nutans*

This is the best time for sowing annuals that have to be sown in place. Elm and elder in leaf. Ash and willow flower.

'Daffodils may be purchased in quantity in many beautiful kinds for a small sum, yet it is a dangerous pastime to study such a publication as Barr's *Catalogue of Daffodils*. One is far too apt literally to take Mahomet's advice – "He that has two cakes of bread, let him sell one of them for some flowers of the Narcissus, for bread is food for the body, but Narcissus is the food of the soul." '
Harry Roberts *The Chronicle of a Cornish Garden* 1901

Sweet violet, *Viola odorata*

**St Patrick's Day. Shamrock worn by the Irish.
Marsh marigold in flower.**

17

'Peas (*Pisum sativum*) are the first seeds planted in
a Boston garden. A local saying calls for planting
them on St Patrick's Day, 17 March, even though
the ground is cold and often blanketed with a
fresh snowfall.'
Sam Bass Warner, Jr *To Dwell Is To Garden* 1987

'In all eastern countries, the Violet is a favourite
flower, and a sherbet flavoured with its blossoms
is a common drink at Persian and Arabian
banquets. The Romans, also, were extremely
partial to the Violet, and cultivated it largely in
their gardens. A favourite beverage of theirs was
a wine made from the flower. It was formerly
commonly believed in England that when Violets
and Roses flourished in Autumn, there would be
some epidemic in the ensuing year. To dream of
admiring the Violet in a garden is deemed
a prognostic of advancement in life.'
Richard Folkard *Plant Lore, Legends and Lyrics* 1884

Great Leopard's Bane, *Doronicum pardalianches*

**After the middle of the month grass seed can
be sown if you want to make a lawn or new
grass paths or to patch bare places in an old
lawn.**

18

'Little think'st thou, poore flower,
Whom I have watchd sixe or seaven dayes,
And seene thy birth, and seene what every houre
Gave to thy growth, thee to this height to raise,
And now dost laugh and triumph on this bough,
Little think'st thou
That it will freeze anon, and that I shall
To morrow finde thee falne, or not at all.'
John Donne 1573–1631 *The Blossom*

19

Yellow Star of Bethlehem, *Ornithogalum luteum*

The globe artichoke can be increased in March. Common elm comes into flower.

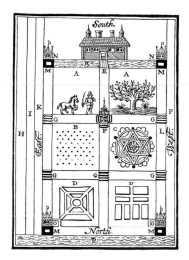

'What can your eye desire to see, your ears to hear, your mouth to take, or your nose to smell, that is not to be had in an Orchard, with abundance of variety? What more delightsome than an infinite variety of sweet smelling flowers, decking with sundry colours, the green mantle of the earth, the universal mother of us all, so by them bespotted, so died, that all the World cannot sample them, and wherein it is more fit to admire the Dyer, than imitate his Workmanship, colouring not only the earth, but decking the air, and sweetning every breath and spirit.'
William Lawson *A New Orchard and Garden* 1618

20

Dog's Violet, *Viola canina*

Shake your nut trees to let the pollen from the catkins fertilize the red flowers which will be out this month.

'In spring time you may delight yourself by culling a few violets – which I will never be without, as long as I can keep a rod or two of garden ground – and placing them in a glass dish, in which there is a little wet silver-sand. The short stems stuck into the sand get sufficient moisture, and a glass over the whole confines the fragrance, so that whenever you are inclined to inhale a full breath of unadulterated violet perfume, you have but to lift off the glass, and enjoy it to your heart's content.'
Shirley Hibberd *Rustic Adornments for Homes of Taste* 1856

Bulbous Fumitory, *Fumaria bulbosa*

Aries: 21 March–20 April. Lawns that have been established for some time should be rolled at this season.

21

'First, sturdy March with brows full sternly bent,
And armed strongly, rode upon a Ram,
The same which over Hellespontus swam:
Yet in his hand a spade he also hent,
And in a bag all sorts of seeds ysame,
Which on the earth he strowed as he went,
And fild her wombe with fruitfull hope of
      nourishment.'
Edmund Spenser *Faerie Queene* 1611

Pilewort, *Ficaria verna*

Ivy growing on walls will benefit considerably if carefully clipped and cleaned. Linnets commence to sing.

22

'We have heard it said, that the labourer who toils in his garden, expends the strength which should be husbanded for his master's service: to which cold-blooded dictate of a heart worthy of a slave-owner, we reply that all experience demonstrates that those laboureres, who devote their leisure to their own gardens, are invariably the best characters and the best workmen in a parish.'
George W. Johnson *The Gardeners's Almanack for 1844*

23

Peerless Daffodil, *Narcissus incomparabilis*

John Bartram born in 1699 in Marple, near Darby, Pennsylvania; laid out a botanical garden by the Schuylkill River, three miles from Philadelphia; became a professional plant collector.

'The seed thee sent last fall was choice good and most of them come up. The ranunculus and anemone root grow finely and several bore fine flowers. The flags – iris – grow well and two of the bulbous is ready to flower. Many aconites is come up and the polianthus by hundreds. Balm of Gilead and a pretty annual linaria hath been long in flower, sowed last February. I hope the yellow digitalis and double-blossom celandine is come up. But how glad, glad should I be if the doronicum gentian and laurels would come up which I sowed carefully last winter under shelter. John Bartram *Letter to Peter Collinson* 1760

24

Golden Saxifrage, *Chrysosplenium oppositifolium*

Dig and clean the ground between your gooseberries and currants, which will strengthen their blossoms, and encourage the trees, and add neatness to the place.

'Gooseberries are very much infested with a small green caterpillar, which frequently devour both leaves and fruit. You must, therefore, be very attentive, and observe their first appearance on the bushes; for, if not destroyed early, they will increase so fast, that they will soon devour all the leaves, and the fruit will then be good for nothing. They make their first appearance generally on the edges and under sides of the leaves.'
John Abercrombie *Every Man His Own Gardener* 1767

Marigold, *Calendula officinalis*

25

**This plant received the Latin name *Calendula*
because it was in flower on the calends of
nearly every month. Until the year 1752, this
was the first month in our calendar, and its
25th day the first of the year.**

'Grief. Although by itself, however, the Marigold
expresses grief, by a judicious mixture with other
flowers its meaning may be greatly varied. For
instance, combined with roses it is symbolic of
"the bitter sweets and pleasant pains of love";
whilst among Eastern nations a bouquet of
marigolds and poppies signifies "I will allay your
pain". Associated with cypress, the emblem of
death, marigolds betoken despair.'
The Language of Flowers 19th Century

Night-shade Leafed Henbane, *Hyoscyamus scopalia*

26

**Plantations of artichokes may be made about
the middle or end of the month, according to
the forwardness of the season. Thrushes and
blackbirds nesting.**

'Faire pledges of a fruitfull Tree,
Why do yee fall so fast?
Your date is not so past;
But you may stay yet here a while,
To blush and gently smile;
And go at last.'
Robert Herrick *To Blossoms* 1648

27

Sweet Jonquil, *Narcissus odorus*

Arrival of the stone curlew. Jackdaws nesting.

'At once, array'd
In all the colours of the flushing year,
By Nature's swift and secret-working hand,
The garden glows, and fills the liberal air
With lavish fragrance; while the promis'd fruit
Lies yet a little embryo, unperceiv'd,
Within its crimson folds.'
James Thomson 1700–48 *The Seasons*

28

Leopard's Bane, *Doronicum plantagineum*

Cut back all newly planted shrubs that flower on the young wood.

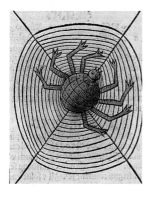

'About this time spiders begin to appear in the gardens, for in winter they are only seen in houses; the species which inhabits our dwellings, is quite distinct from the gardening spider....Naturalists have found out this curious propensity in spiders, that they seem remarkably fond of music, and have been know to descend from the ceiling during concerts, and to retire when the strain was finished.'
T. Forster *Perennial Calendar* 1824

Oxlip or Great Cowslip, *Primula elatior*

29

Rhubarb. This wholesome and agreeable vegetable has become so popular as a substitute for fruit in early spring that no garden should be without it.

'All the grass that is cut off, when mowing the lawn, should be made into a neat pile on the rubbish heap. After this pile has been left to rot for six months it will give us a valuable supply of humus that can be dug into the soil in Winter.'
Edward R. Anson *The Small Garden* 1936

'Now 'tis the spring, and weeds are shallow
    rooted;
Suffer them now and they'll o'ergrow the garden,
And choke the herbs for want of husbandry.'
William Shakespeare *Henry VI Part 2* 1592

Water-cress, *Cardamine hirsuta*

30

All hybrid perpetual roses should be pruned at the end of March. Wheatear and chiffchaff arrive about this time.

'Of wilde water-Cresses or Cuckow-floures. The first of the Cuckow flours hath leaves at his springing up somwhat round, & those that spring afterward grow jagged like the leaves of Greek Valerian; among which riseth a stalk a foot long, set with the like leaves, but smaller and more jagged, resembling those of Rocket. The floures grow at the top in small bundles, white of colour, hollow in the middle, resembling the white sweet-John: after which come small chaffie huskes or seed-vessels, wherein the seed is contained. The root is small and threddy. These floure for the most part in Aprill and May, when the Cuckow begins to sing her pleasant notes without stammering.'
John Gerard *Herball* 1597

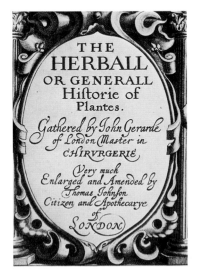

THE
HERBALL
OR GENERALL
Hiſtorie of
Plantes.

Gathered by John Gerarde of London (Maſter in CHIRVRGERIE

Very much Enlarged and Amended by Thomas Johnſon Citizen and Apothecarye of LONDON

31

Benjamin Tree, *Laurus benzoin*

Arrival of the least willow wren. Wych elm in flower.

'As for the Times and Seasons of the Year, from the beginning to the end thereof, every day something is to be done by the Husbandman; as was said of a Gardiner, that his work is never at an end, it begins with the Year, and continues to the next. Yet is it not every year alike, neither is every place alike; some years, or at least some seasons of the year, prove more forward by two or three weeks, or more, at one time than another.'
John Worlidge *Kalendarium Rusticum* 1675

APRIL

called *Aperire*, because in this Month the Earth
begins to bring forth Fruits.
Temperature: 47.1° Fahrenheit (8.4° Celsius).
Rainfall: 1.76 inches (4.5 cm).

1

French Annual Mercury, *Mercurialis annua*

The first three days of April are frequently very stormy. This month requires the greatest exertions of any in the year with the gardener, the ground being ready to receive whatever is planted or sown.

'In April follow the double white Violet, the Wallflower, the Stock-Gilliflower, the Cowslip, Flower-de-Luces, and Lilies of all natures; Rosemary-flowers, the Tulip, the double Peony, the pale Daffodil, the French Honeysuckle, the Cherry-tree in blossom, the Damascene and Plum-trees in blossom, the White Thorn in leaf, the Lilac-tree.'
Francis Bacon *Of Gardens* 1625

2

White Violet, *Viola alba*

From 1860 onward Scotland became peculiarly the home of the cultivated pansy. Wrens nesting.

'In England it is thought that if any one kills a wren or harries its nest, he will infallibly break a bone or meet with some dreadful misfortune within the year; sometimes it is thought that the cows will give bloody milk.'
J. G. Frazer *The Golden Bough* 1890

Evergreen Alkanet, *Anchusa sempervivens*

3

**This is the best time to plant evergreens.
Swallows arrive.**

'The value of wood-ashes for fruit-trees. In
England, a private dwelling is not considered
complete without an ash-vault; and a good farmer
would dispense with his barn rather than be
destitute of an ash-house. I have known farmers
to supply the cottagers with as much peat as they
could burn, on condition of their saving them the
ashes; and there are some that will keep men under
pay throughout the year burning peat for the same
purpose; and anything that has passed the fire is so
valuable, that a chimney-sweep will frequently clean
chimneys for the sake of the soot, which is
conveyed miles into the country, and sold at a price
sufficient to reward the collectors, besides paying
all expenses.'
S. Edwards Todd *The American Gardener's Assistant* 1867

Red Crown Imperial, *Fritillaria imperialis*

4

**Fertilize peaches, nectarines and apricots by
passing a rabbit's tail from flower to flower.**

'Although divers learned men do by the name
given unto this delightfull plant, thinke it doth in
forme things partake with a Tulipa or Daffodil,
and have therefore placed it betweene them; yet
I, finding it most like unto a little Lilly, both in
roote, stalke, leafe, and flower, and seede, have
(as you see here) placed it next unto the Lillies,
and before them. Hereof there are many sorts
found out of late, as white, red, blacke, and
yellow, besides the purple, which was first
knowne. I have not found or heard by any others
on any property peculiar in this plant, to be
applied either inwardly or outwardly for any
disease: the chiefe or onely use thereof is, to be
an ornament for the Gardens of the curious
lovers of these delights.'
John Parkinson *Paradisus* 1629

5

Yellow Crown Imperial, *Fritillaria imperialis lutea*

Grass, whether a lawn or path, may be mown about once a fortnight in April.

'For some reason the English cottager is not good to his grass plot. Now and then we see the turf cared for as it should be, but as a rule it is neglected, weed-grown, and unkempt. The practice of leaving things to themselves, so often productive of charm where hardy flower borders and free-growing climbers are concerned, is fatal to the appearance of a lawn, which can only be beautiful when regularly tended. Nothing degenerates more quickly than once-mown turf; nothing gives a garden a sadder or more desolate aspect. If all culture were suspended for a year among the beds and borders and only the grass was regularly rolled, cut, and swept, the garden would still look a garden; the idea that it was used and appreciated, that labour was given cheerfully, would still prevail.'
Charles Thonger *The Book of the Cottage Garden* 1908

6

Starch Hyacinth, *Hyacinthus racemosus*

Carrots, if not already in, must be sown now and need a very sandy soil, so if your ground is heavy dig in plenty of road grit.

'A substitute for mowing with the scythe has lately been introduced in the form of a mowing-machine, which requires far less skill and exertion than the scythe, and answers perfectly where the surface of the soil to be mowed is perfectly smooth and firm, the grass of even quality, and the machine only used in dry weather. It is particularly adapted for amateurs, affording an excellent exercise to the arms and every part of the body; but it is proper to observe that many gardeners are prejudiced against it.'
Jane Loudon *The Ladies' Companion to the Flower Garden* 1841

Wood Anemone, *Anemone nemorosa*

7

The poet William Wordsworth born in 1770 in Cockermouth, Cumberland; he designed the gardens at Dove Cottage from 1799 and at Royal Mount from 1813.

'Laying out grounds, as it is called, may be considered as a liberal art, in some sort like poetry and painting; and its object, like that of all the liberal arts, is, or ought to be, to move the affections under the control of good sense. If this be so when we are merely putting together words or colours, how much more ought the feeling to prevail when we are in the midst of the realities of things; of the beauty and harmony, of the joy and happiness of living creatures; of men and children, of birds and beasts, of hills and streams, and trees and flowers, with the changes of night and day, evening and morning, summer and winter, and all their unwearied actions and energies.'
William Wordsworth *Letter to Sir G. Beaumont* 1805

Ground Ivy, *Glechoma hederacea*

8

John Claudius Loudon born in 1783 in Cambuslang, Lanarkshire; horticultural writer and editor who conceived the 'gardenesque' style of planting; designed gardens and cemeteries; invented the wrought-iron glazing bar for curvilinear glasshouse.

'It is said that the browsing of a goat gave the first idea of pruning the vine; as chance, which had set fire to a rose tree, according to Acosta, gave the first idea of pruning the rose. Theophrastus informs us that without that precaution they would bear no flowers.'
John Loudon *The Encyclopaedia of Gardening* 1822

9

Red Polyanthus, *Primula*

Polyanthus and coloured primroses may be sown now in a sheltered place in drills. Queen wasps emerge from hibernation.

'In the spring of the yeare joy springs afresh in beholding the seeds, and young Grafts and Plants spring forth vigorously and strongly. And the buds and blossomes breathing forth pretious and pleasant Oders, rejoyce and delight the inward and outward senses, promising a plentiful Harvest of Fruits in Autumne; and all the Sommer long joy is cherished, with coole fresh ayres, singing Birds, sight of abundance of Fruits, burd'ning all the Trees, delighting the Eye with their beautifull formes and colours; and in Autumne joy is renewed againe with a rich and plentiful Harvest of Fruits; and all the Winter long joy is nourished and fed with a free use of all the Fruits, and Wines, and Delicates made of them. So here's a succession of joyes… conducing to Long-life.'
Ralph Austen *A Treatise of Fruit-Trees* 1653

10

Pale Violet, *Viola tombrigens*

The ashes that result from the garden bonfire should be carefully preserved, for they are invaluable, especially for mixing with heavy soil when planting out sweet peas, gladioli, and many other plants that are put out in the spring.

'Planting and Gardening addes much to the Health and Content of Man.'
Moses Cook *The Manner of Raising, Ordering, and Improving Forrest-Trees* 1676

'Buried an old hen at the foot of a plum-tree by the light of the full moon – am told it will then bear egg-plums.'
George Cruikshank *Comic Almanack* 1855

Dandelion, *Leontodon taraxacum*

11

**More springs in the garden than the gardener
ever sowed. Chaffinches build their nests.
Hedgehogs again active after winter
hibernation.**

'The first mention of the Dandelion as
a medicine is in the works of the Arabian
physicians of the tenth and eleventh centuries,
who speak of it as a sort of wild Endive, under
the name of Taraxacon. In this country, we find
allusion to it in the Welsh medicines of the
thirteenth century. Dandelion was much valued
as a medicine in the times of Gerard and
Parkinson, and is still extensively employed.
Dandelion roots have long been largely used on
the Continent, and the plant is cultivated largely
in India as a remedy for liver complaints.'
Mrs M. Grieve *A Modern Herbal* 1931

Great Thick-leafed Saxifrage, *Saxifraga crassifloia*

12

**Much foresight is needed in spring; we are so
apt to forget to sow or plant till we see the
flower we wish in another person's garden.**

'The several kinds of Marigolds begin their
Blossoms in April, and continue 'till the Winter's
cold destroys them; and as they are continually
blowing and decaying, so they are continually
succeeded by crooked Seeds, which may be
sown as soon as ripe, or any time in the Spring.'
Batty Langley *New Principles of Gardening* 1728

'Magnolia stellata is an invaluable shrub which
we owe to Japan. It bears white flowers all over
the branches and in April is one of the most
decorative shrubs in the garden.'
Samuel Graveson *My Villa Garden* 1915

13

Green Narcissus, *Narcissus viridiflorus*

Thomas Jefferson born in 1743 in Shadwell, Virginia; President of USA 1801-09; visited England in 1786 and wrote *Memorandums made on a tour to some of the Gardens in England.*

'I have often thought that if heaven had given me choice of my position and calling, it should have been on a rich spot of earth, well watered, and near a good market for the production of the garden. No occupation is so delightful to me as the culture of the earth, and no culture comparable to that of the garden. Such a variety of subjects, some one alway comming to perfection, the failure of one thing repaired by the success of another, and instead of one harvest a continued one through the year. Under a total want of demand except for our family table, I am still devoted to the garden. But though an old man, I am but a young gardener.'
Thomas Jefferson *Garden Book* 1766–1824

14

Common Borage, *Borago officinalis*

Arrival of the nightingale. Blackthorn in flower. Lesser white butterfly arrives.

'Borage is a great favourite with the honey-bee. We have sown the seeds extensively in some years, and valued it, not only because we saw our honey-gathering friends continually busied about its flowers, but for the beautiful blue colour of the large blossoms, which greatly ornamented our grounds.'
Robert Tyas *The Language of Flowers* 1869

Greater Stitchwort, *Stellaria holostea*

Arrival of the chimney swallow, yellow willow wren and pied flycatcher.

15

'I fail to see why every man who has ground enough to plant half-a-dozen Apple trees should not do so; in fact, I should like to see every cottage gardener turn his attention more than is now done to fruit culture, not only to supply the wants of his family, but also where favourably situated for the purpose of adding to his income.'
Edward Hobday *Cottage Gardening* 1877

'The Moone hath no such influence upon fruit-trees. Men (we see by experience) graft in all seasons of the Moon, and find no such difference in the bearing of the trees.'
Ralph Austen *A Treatise of Fruit-Trees* 1653

Yellow Tulip, *Tulipa sylvestris*

Arrival of the redstart and grasshopper lark. Crabapple in bloom.

16

'One chief charm of a garden, I think, depends on surprise. There is a kind of dulness in Tulips and Hyacinths, sorted, and coming up all one size and colour. I love to watch the close-folded Tulip bud, rising higher and higher daily – almost hourly – from its brown bed; and never to be quite certain of the colour that is to be, till one morning I find the rose, or golden, or ruby cup in all its finished beauty; perhaps not at all what was expected. And then, amid these splendours, will suddenly appear one shorter or taller than the rest, of the purest, rarest white. How that white Tulip, coming as it were by chance, is valued!'
Mrs Boyle *Days and Hours in a Garden* 1884

17

Friar's-cowl, Broad-leafed Arum, *Arum arisarum*

Arrival of the blackcap, whinchat and whitethroat.

'For my part, notwithstanding I have been about Forty Years in the Business of Gardening, I find the Art so mysterious that the whole Life of a Man may be employ'd in it, without gaining a true knowledge of every Thing necessary to be done. I and others have seen Plants that were to be sold in the Markets, that were as uncertain of Growth as a Piece of Noah's Ark would be, had we it here to plant.'
Thomas Fairchild *The City Gardener* 1722

18

Musk Narcissus, *Narcissus moschato*

Goslings become common. Sedge warbler arrives.

'Talke of perfect happinesse or pleasure, and what place was so fit for that as the garden place wherein Adam was set to be the Herbarist? Whither did the Poets hunt for their sincere delights, but into the gardens of Alcinous, of Adonis, and the Orchards of the Hesperides? Where did they dreame that heaven should be, but in the pleasant garden of Elysium? Whither doe all men walke for their honest recreation, but thither where the earth hath most beneficially painted her face with flourishing colours? And what season of the yeare more longed for than the Spring, whose gentle breath inticeth forth the kindly sweets, and makes them yeeld their fragrant smells?'
John Gerard *Herball* 1597

Garlic, *Allium ursinum*

19

Arrival of the martlet and spotted flycatcher.

'Sith Garlick then hath poure to save from death,
Beare with it though it make unsavoury breath:
And scorne not Garlick like to some, that think
It onely makes men winke, and drinke, and stink.'
John Harington *The Englishman's Doctor* 1607

'The Leaves of Parsley eaten after Onyons Leekes
or Garlick, taketh away the offensive smell of
them.'
William Coles *Adam in Eden: or, Natures Paradise* 1657

Spring Snowflake, *Leucojum vernum*

20

**The spring snowflake flowers about this time,
and is an elegant successor of the early
snowdrop, now no longer seen.**

'Many people express their horror of garlic who
have never tasted it, and who would not
recognise the plant if laid before them; but who
also relish samples of London and Parisian
cookery, which they would refuse if aware of the
ingredient that serves to heighten the flavour of
the sauce. Prejudices in eating and drinking are
exceedingly difficult to eradicate; and untried
articles of diet are the objects of the strongest
prejudice. But garlic being in great repute as
a tonic and stomachich antidote to the debility
caused by long-continued hot weather, is also
recommended as affording relief to nervous,
hysterical, and convulsive affections.'
E. S. Delamer *The Kitchen Garden* 1855

21

Cypress Narcissus, *Narcissus orientalis albus*

Taurus: 21 April–21 May. Arrival of the cuckoo, sandpiper and great green willow wren.

'Now Lasses into Groves and Meadows gets,
To gather Primroses and Violets;
But let them heed they do not too far stray,
Lest they their Maiden-heads do lose that way.'
Poor Robin 1691

'If you will sprinkle your fruit-trees in the spring, by the help of a garden engine, or other means, with soap suds, twice a week for two or three weeks, you will soon find that caterpillars and canker worms are as scarce on your premises as musquitoes in December.'
Thomas Green Fessenden *The New England Farmer's Almanack for 1828*

22

Wood Crowfoot or Goldilocks, *Ranunculus auri comus*

Potatoes should be earthed up slightly, where showing, to protect against frost. Grasshopper warbler and lesser whitethroat arrive.

'Ashes near, but not in contact with bulbs is advised when they are menaced by mice.'
Louise Shelton *Continuous Blooms in America* 1915

'Insects in green-house devouring all my new plants; searched book for a remedy, and last night, popped in a pan of burning brimstone. This morning all the grubs shrivelled to shreds, and every plant dead and stripped as naked as a plucked chicken.'
George Cruikshank *Comic Almanack* 1835

Harebell, *Hyacinthus non scriptus*

23

**St George's Day. Fashion of wearing blue
coats on St George's Day probably because
blue was the national colour of Britain, and
not in imitation of the clothing of the fields
in blue by the flowering of an abundance
of bluebells, as some have supposed.**

'In Aprill about S. George his day, you shall set
abroad your citron and orange trees, as also all
such other trees as you had kept within house
from S. Martins day.'
Richard Surflet *The Countrie Farme* 1600

Blackthorn, *Prunus spinosa*

24

**Never turn out tender, or even half-hardy,
plants until the middle or end of May.
Wood warbler arrives.**

'If a garden isn't shaggy, forget it.'
Derek Jarman *Derek Jarman's Garden* 1995

'Gardeners get a double supply of pleasure,
for always, while they are enjoying the actuality
of the present and its blossoming, in
imagination they enjoy in their planning the
flowering of future plants.'
Clare Leighton *Four Hedges* 1935

25

Clarimond Tulip, *Tulipa praecox*

Each year about 3 billion Dutch tulips are sold and planted. There are more than 3500 distinct varieties of tulips available.

'In mild weather Tulips may stand abroad, and may be allowed to receive a soft shower, but must be screened from heavy rains; they will require little or no water, and while in flower, must be sheltered from rains. The Garden Tulip is a native of the Levant; Linnaeus says, of Cappadocia. It is very common in Syria; and is supposed, by some persons, to be the lily of the field alluded to by Jesus Christ. In Persia where it grows in abundance, it is considered as the emblem of perfect lovers.'
Elizabeth Kent *Flora Domestica* 1823

26

Yellow Erysimum, *Erysimum barbarea*

Arrival of the sand martin and corncrake.

'I, Borage, always bring Courage'
Latin saying

'When I behoulde upon a barraine, dry and deserted earth, such as the Peake-hills, where a man may behould snow all summer, or on the East-mores, whose best hearbage is nothing but mosse, and iron stone, in such a place, I say, to behoulde a delicate, rich, and fruitful garden, it shewes great worthiness in the owner, and infinite Art and industry in the workeman, and makes us both admire and love the begetters of such excellencies.'
Gervase Markham *The English Husbandman* 1613

Great Daffodil, *Narcissus major*

27

Window plants often suffer considerable damage at this time of year from drying out. Turtle dove arrives.

'So twice five miles of fertile ground
With walls and towers were girdled round:
And there were gardens bright with sinuous rills,
Where blossomed many an incense-bearing tree;
And here were forests ancient as the hills,
Enfolding sunny spots of greenery.'
Samuel Taylor Coleridge *Kubla Khan* 1798

Spotted Arum, *Arum maculatum*

28

In 1770 Captain Cook and Joseph Banks landed in Australia at Sting Ray Bay, later to be called Botany Bay because of the large number of plants found there.

'Sweete Aprill showers,
do spring May flowers.'
Thomas Tusser *Five Hundreth Points of Good Husbandry* 1573

'About the seasons of the year,
Astrologers may make a fuss;
But this I know, that spring is here
When I can eat asparagus.'
Poor Robin 1808

29

Herb Robert, *Geranium robertianum*

Floralia in the Roman calendar. Dragon-fly appears. Garden warbler and swifts arrive.

'Flora was the goddess of flowers and gardens among the Romans, the same as the Chloris of the Greeks. Some suppose that she was a common courtesan, who left to the Romans the immense riches which she had acquired by prostitution and lasciviousness; in remembrance of which a yearly festival was instituted in her honour. She was worshipped even among the Sabines long before the foundation of Rome. It is said that she married Zephyrus, and that she received from him the privilege of presiding over flowers, and of enjoying perpetual youth. She was represented as crowned with flowers, and holding in her hand the horn of plenty.'
T. Forster *The Perennial Calendar* 1824

30

Cowslip, *Primula veris*

Cowslip wine is pleasant and said to be slightly narcotic. Holly blue butterflies appear.

'And after April, when May follows,
And the whitethroat builds, and all the swallows!
Hark, where my blossomed pear-tree in
the hedge
Leans to the field and scatters on the clover
Blossoms and dewdrops – at the bent
spray's edge –
That's the wise thrush; he sings each song
twice over,
Lest you should think he never could recapture
The first fine careless rapture!
And though the fields look rough with
hoary dew,
All will be gay when noontide wakes anew
The buttercups, the little children's dower
– Far brighter than this gaudy melon-flower!'
Robert Browning *Home-Thoughts, from Abroad* 1845

MAY

comes from *Majus*. It was dedicated to the oldest
Citizens of Rome, who were called Majores.
Temperature: 52.7° Fahrenheit (11.5° Celsius).
Rainfall: 2.07 inches (5 cm).

1

Gesner Tulip, *Tulipa gesneriana*

In 1890 the first political May Day celebrations in England took place in Hyde Park. They were part of the campaign for the eight-hour day and up to half a million people marched to the park.

'May, the Milk-month of our Saxon ancestors, is said to have derived its name from the pastoral custom of English maidens – the Mays of our older authors – of rising early on May morning, and proceeding to the meadows to milk the cows, and elect the most beautiful of their companions as the "Queen of the Mays". In process of time, when the name was established, and the custom in which it originated had become a tradition, another May-day custom had crept in, when, according to old Herrick,

Not a budding boy or girl that day,
But is got up and gone to bring in May.'
Samuel Orchart Beeton *The Book of Garden Management* 1862

2

Charlock, *Raphanus raphanistrum*

Asparagus will now be fit for gathering for use. Horse-chestnut and mountain ash in flower.

'He that would live for aye,
Must eat sage in May.'
Old English saying

'Put Sage in drinke, drinke Worme-wood-wine,
Use Physickes helpe, walke mornings fine.'
John Neve *A New Almanack* 1641

Poetic Narcissus, *Narcissus poeticus*

3

Now is the time to plant the window boxes. Nightjar arrives. Caterpillars will now be hatching.

'During the many years I lived in the hill country of New York I was glad every year when May came round that just beyond my chamber window grew a white Hawthorn tree. It made an entrancing event of awakening, for its perfume entered the room with the first morning breeze.'
Louise Beebe Wilder *The Fragrant Path* 1932

Stock Gillyflower, *Cheiranthus incanus*

4

Where apricots and peaches are too thick, they should be thinned the beginning of this month, observing never to leave two or more fruit together, as is too often practised by covetous persons.

'I suppose there will always be a craze for "bigness", even in the garden. Whilst I can forgive the grower of the big gooseberry, potato and tomato, for I know that both mouths and stomachs differ in size, I find it a harder matter to forgive the flower hybridist who puts bigness before grace. When I recall the strange mop-looking things exhibited as chrysanthemums, the magenta pincushions known as Dahlias and the weedy, discoloured Decipiens Saxifrages, I confess to a belief that certain gardeners must have fallen from grace.'
Samuel Graveson *My Villa Garden* 1915

5

Apple-tree, *Pyrus malus*

Deadhead spring bulbs. Orange-tip butterflies appear.

'5 May 1774. A frost which destroyed almost everything. It killed the wheat, rye, corn, many tobacco plants, and even large saplings. The leaves of the trees were entirely killed. All the shoots of vines. At Monticello near half the fruit of every kind was killed; and before this no instance had ever occurred of any fruit killed here by the frost. In all other places in the neighbourhood the destruction of fruit was total. This frost was general and equally destructive thro the whole country and the neighbouring colonies.'

Thomas Jefferson *Garden Book 1766–1824*

6

Bright Yellow Globe-flower, *Trollius europaeus*

In 1831 there was a severe frost in England. The thermometer fell to 26 [° Fahrenheit], or 6 degrees below freezing.

'Farewell, a long farewell, to all my greatness!
This is the state of man: today he puts forth
The tender leaves of hope, tomorrow blossoms,
And bears his blushing honours thick upon him:
The third day comes a frost, a killing frost,
And – when he thinks, good easy man, full surely
His greatness is a-ripening – nips his root,
And then he falls, as I do.'

William Shakespeare *King Henry VIII* 1613

Bright Orange Asiatic Globe-flower, *Trollius asiaticus*

Beds of tulips begin to flower.

7

'"Here they are! blowing, growing, all alive!" This was an old London cry by little flower gardeners, who brought the products of their grounds to the metropolis, and wheeled them through the streets in a barrow, "blowing, growing, all alive!" to tempt purchasers in the humble streets and alleys of working neighbourhoods. Acts of Parliament have put down the flower-pots, which were accustomed to "topple on the *walkers'* heads", from the windows of houses, wherein flower-fanciers dwelt.'
William Hone *The Every-Day Book* 1830

Lily of the Valley, *Convalaria majalis*

**Continue to make sowings of spinach.
Hawthorn in bloom.**

8

'*The Lily of the Valley*, sometimes called the May Lily, and in some country villages Ladder to Heaven, in the floral languages of Europe is emblematic of the *return to happiness*, doubtless in allusion to the season of the year when it puts forth its blossoms.'
The Language of Flowers 19th Century

9

Lily of the Valley, *Convalaria multiflora*

On 9 May 1831 there was an extraordinary snow storm in the west part of New York. Snow fell to the depth of 10 or 12 inches.

'The naiad-like lily of the vale,
Whom youth makes so fair, and passion so pale,
That the light of its tremulous bells is seen
Through their pavilions of tender green.'
Percy Bysshe Shelley *The Sensitive Plant* 1820

10

Slender-leafed Peony, *Paeonia tenuifolia*

About the tenth is the best time to sow carnation seeds. Cuckoo-spit insect appears. Lady's mantle in flower.

'An army of shrubs and plants give of their best during May; cherries and flowering crabs are a joy, lilacs and laburnum play no small part, great full-blown paeonies and the single-flowered of their kind, and, loveliest of all, the great tree paeonies of Japan. The paeony species are exquisitely beautiful, and some of these deserve to be far more widely grown.'
Herbert Cowley *The Garden Year* 1936

Lancashire Asphodel, *Asphodelus luteus*

11

**Sage, set slips in May, and they grow aye;
let it not seed, it will last longer. Hazel in
leaf.**

'The little garden is crowded with a medley of
old-fashioned herbs and flowers, planted long
ago, when the garden was the only druggist's
shop within reach, and allowed to grow in
scrambling and wild luxuriance – roses,
lavender, sage, balm (for tea), rosemary, pinks
and wallflowers, onions and jessamine, in most
republican and indiscriminate order.'
Elizabeth Gaskell *Mary Barton* 1848

German Iris, *Iris germanica*

12

**The foliage of trees is commonly completed
by this time. It begins with the aquatic kinds,
such as the willow, poplar and alder, proceeds
to the lime, sycamore and horse-chestnut, and
concludes with the oak, beech, ash, walnut
and mulberry, these last, however, are seldom
in full leaf till June.**

'The German Iris, *Iris Germanica*, has been
completely stripped of its Teutonic character
– if it ever had one. It has regularly come into
favour, and is one of the very best plants for
town gardens.'
George Taylor *British Garden Flowers* 1946

'I have seen almost every little peach or apricot
in a garden killed stone dead in this week; and
these young set fruits are, in my experience, at
least as sensitive to frost as the flowers.'
William Beach Thomas *An Observer's Twelvemonth*
1923

13

Common Comfrey, *Symphytum officinalis*

Soot is useful to keep off slugs in the herbaceous border.

'The days of "the three Icemen", St Pancratius, Servatius, and Bonifacius, fall on May 12th, 13th and 14th respectively. This is perhaps the most regular of all the seasonable spells of weather. Again and again at this period, if not exactly on these days, come the last frosts, and they are feared more than any other weather event in the year. Fruit bloom – strawberry and early apple and late plum – is at its tenderest, as are many newly sprung shoots of rose or dielytra or potato.'
W. Beach Thomas and A. K. Collett *The English Year* 1913

14

Common Peony, *Paeonia officinalis*

The dandelion now presents the curious spectacle of a crop of blowers, as children call them, from the large balls of plumed seed which their numerous stalks bear.

'Colette says, "The peony smells of peonies, that is to say of cockchafers," and only she would know what cockchafers smell like. Lilacs, she further says, have the "discreet smell of scarab beetles," whatever that may be. I am not good at such comparisons. Peony scents vary greatly, from one so like a rose I couldn't in the dark tell the difference, to an acrid sweetness not unlike the lilac's.'
Eleanor Perenyi *Green Thoughts* 1981

Welsh Poppy, *Papaver cambricum*

15

If the weather is mild and settled sow French beans. Wood-white butterfly appears. Lilacs in flower.

'If to a man there betide much wakefulness, rub down a poppy in oil, smear thy forehead therewith and all thy body, wonderfully soon the wakefulness will be moderated for him.'
Leech Book of Bald 10th Century

'The Garden Beanes serve more for the use of the poore than of the rich. They are only boyled in faire water and a little salt, and afterwards stewed with some butter, a little vinegar and pepper being put unto them, and so eaten. The water of the blossoms distilled is used to take away spots, and to cleer the skin.'
John Parkinson *Paradisus* 1629

Great Star of Bethlehem, *Ornithogalum umbellatum*

16

More birds sing in May than in any other month in the year. Fertilize the lawn.

'When apple-trees in blossoms are,
And cherries of a silken white,
And king-cups deck the meadows fair,
And daffodils in brooks delight;
When golden wallflowers bloom around,
And purple violets scent the ground,
And lilac 'gins to shew her bloom, -
We then may say the May is come.'
John Clare 1793–1864

17

Long Rough-headed, Early Red Poppy, *Papaver argemone*

Comfrey now coming into flower. Take cuttings of aubrieta, arabis and alyssum as soon as the flowers are over.

'There is no flower can be more glorious than the Poppy, were it as good as great, and as sweet as well coloured, and as lasting as it is nimble in growth, but their ill smell and soon fading makes them less regarded.'
John Worlidge *The Art of Gardening* 1677

'A swarm of bees in May
Is worth a load of hay.'
Traditional rhyme

18

Mouse-ear or Hawkweed, *Hieracium pilosella*

William Thompson born in 1823 in Ipswich, Suffolk; founded the nursery in Ipswich, later known as Thompson and Morgan.

'The love of flowers is a sentiment common alike to the great and to the little; to the old and to the young; to the learned and the ignorant; the illustrious and the obscure. While the simplest child may take delight in them, they may also prove a recreation to the most profound philosophers.'
Elizabeth Kent *Flora Domestica* 1823

Monk's Hood, *Aconitum napellus*

19

If gardens are to flourish either for beauty or usefulness, the insect tribes must die. Guelder rose in flower.

'Shakespeare refers twice to the poisonous monkshood (*Aconitum napellus*). In his day it was accounted the most deadly of poisons, for mineral poisons were unknown.'
Eleanour Sinclair Rohde *Shakespeare's Wild Flowers, Fairy Lore, Gardens, Herbs, Gatherers of Simples and Bee Lore* 1935

'African marygold. – If this plant opens not its flowers in the morning about seven o'clock, you may be sure it will rain that day, unless it thunders.'
William Hone *The Every-Day Book* 1830

Horse-chestnut, *Aeschylus hippocastanum*

20

In early years a few roses begin to appear about this time and sweet violets decay. These two flowers have been styled the rivals of spring and are oftener put in contrast than any other.

'Hawthorn. Hope. The flowering of the Hawthorn announces that Winter is over. It generally commences to flower in May. Birds are fond of building their nests in its bushes. The Romans thought that it had the power of keeping them from evil. It was used by them particularly as wedding offerings. In the provinces of France, also a bough is often placed on the cot of an infant to bring good luck.'
Maud Dean *The Language of Flowers* 1897

21

Ragged Robin, *Lychnis flos cuculi*

The poet and essayist Alexander Pope born in 1688 in London; he attacked fashionable topiary and advocated a return to nature, and he created a famous garden at his home in Twickenham.

'I have more fruit-trees and kitchen-garden than you have any thought of; nay I have good Melons and Pine-apples of my own growth. I am as much a better Gardiner, as I'm a worse Poet, than when you saw me.'
Alexander Pope *Letter to Jonathan Swift*
25 March 1736

'My Garden like my Life, seems to me every Year to want Correction and require attention.'
Alexander Pope *Letter to Ralph Allen*
6 November 1736

22

Yellow Star of Bethlehem, *Tragopogon pratensis*

Gemini: 22 May–21 June. Laburnums in blossom. Skipper butterflies appear.

'Star of Bethlehem. It continues to flower during two or three weeks, but never unfolds except in bright sunshine, and even then not before eleven; hence gardeners often call it Eleven-o'clock-Lady.'
Anne Pratt *The Flowering Plants and Ferns of Great Britain* 1855

'Your Bees delight in wood, for feeding, especially for casting, therefore want not an Orchard. A May's swarm is worth a Mares Foal: if they want wood, they be in danger of flying away.'
William Lawson *The Country House-wifes Garden* 1617

Lilac, *Syringa vulgaris*

23

The weather about this time is very apt to become warmer and the cold winds which sometimes blow in May to be changed for more temperate gales; in that case summer seems to come on all at once.

'In America it is the Lilac chiefly that scents the May world, and while nowhere does any species of Syringa grow naturally within the boundaries of our country, it is perhaps the most frequently encountered shrub in all sections where it will grow at all.'
Louise Beebe Wilder *The Fragrant Path* 1932

Monkey Poppy, *Papaver orientalis*

24

Linnaeus born in 1707 in the south of Sweden; invented the binomial system of classifying plants. Great celandine flowers.

'The cultivation of annual flowers is a delightful employment, and well adapted to the amusement of a lady, who, with the assistance of a laborer to prepare the ground, may turn a barren waste into a beauteous flower-garden with her own hands. Sowing the seed, transplanting, watering, and training the plants, tying them to sticks as props, leading them over trellis-work, and gathering their seed, are all suitable feminine occupations; and from their affording motives for exercise in the open air, they contribute greatly to health and tranquillity of mind.'
S. Edwards Todd *The American Gardener's Assistant* 1867

25

Common Herb Bennet, *Geum uranum*

The croaking of frogs more than usual in the evening signifies rain. White ox-eye daisy and Solomon's Seal in flower.

'In this plucking up, and purging of the Garden beds of weeds and stones, the same about the plants ought to be exercised by hand, then with an Iron instrument, for feare of feebling the young plants, yet small and tender of growth. And in the weeding with the hand, the Gardener must diligently take heed that he does not too boisterously loose the earth, nor handle much the plants in plucking away the weeds, but the same purge so tenderly, that the roots of the young plants be not loosed and feebled in the soft earth: for occasion will move the carefull Gardener to weed dainty hearbs, being young and tender, lest grosse weeds in the growing up with them, may annoy and hinder their increasing.'
Thomas Hyll *The Gardener's Labyrinth* 1577

26

Purple Rhododendron, *Rhododendron ponticum*

A few unripe gooseberries begin now to be gathered for tarts, which, however, still taste a good deal of the wood, though they are by some persons regarded as a great luxury.

'Took up my hyacinth bulbs & laid them in ridges of earth to dry – made a new frame for my Ariculas – found a large white orchis in Oxey Wood of a curious species and very rare I watched a Bluecap or Blue Titmouse feeding her young whose nest was in a wall close to an Orchard she got caterpillars out of the Blossoms of the apple trees and leaves of the plumb – she fetched 120 caterpillars in half an hour – now supposing she only feeds them 4 times a day a quarter of an hour each time she fetches in no less than 480 Caterpillars & I should think treble that number.'
John Clare *Journal* 1825

Buttercup, *Ranunculus acris*

If the broom be full of flowers, it usually signifies plenty. Woodruff flowering. Puss moth appears.

'Plants have Brute Enemies. I begin with Dogs and Cats, because they come uppermost in my mind; and affirm, they ought not to be suffer'd in a Flower-Garden. Your Dogs do, by their continual leaping, leave ugly Marks, or Impressions, upon the Surface of the Ground, which spoils it, let us take never so much care to keep it smooth; and Cats scattering their Ordure all about, and then scraping the Earth to cover it, grub up many plants, to the great mortification of all curious Florists.'
Louis Liger d'Auxerre *The Compleat Florist* 1706

27

Lurid Iris, *Iris lurida*

Roses and other flowers – wash with tobacco tea to destroy aphids.

'Hollyhocks had sprung up tall as trees, lilies had opened, tulips and roses were in bloom; the borders of the little beds were gay with pink thrift and crimson double daisies; the sweetbriars gave out, morning and evening, their scent of spice and apples; and these fragrant treasures were all useless for most of the inmates of Lowood, except to furnish now and then a handful of herbs and blossoms to put in a coffin.'
Charlotte Brontë *Jane Eyre* 1847

28

29

Bluebottle, *Centaurea montana*

Oak-apple Day. Place clean straw between strawberry plants to keep the fruit clean.

'To rise betimes will do thee good. Sleepe a littell after dinner.'
William Ram *Little Dodoen* 1606

'Half my time taken up in driving the butterflies off the gooseberry trees. Left my weeding-gloves stuck on a stick last night – put them on this morning, and smashed five slugs in one, and seven earwigs in the other. Mem. Old gloves the best slug-trap.'
George Cruikshank *Comic Almanack 1835*

30

Lesser Spearwort, *Ranunculus flammula*

Ne'er cast a clout till May is out. The surest way to have your seeds grow is to sow such as are not above one year old.

'The Black-bird and Throstle (for I take it, the Thrush sings not, but devours) sing loudly in a May morning, and delights the ear much, and you need not want their company, if you have ripe Cherries or Berries, and would as gladly as the rest do your pleasure: but I had rather want their company than my fruit.'
William Lawson *A New Orchard and Garden* 1618

Yellow Turk's Cap Lily, *Lilium pomponium*

31

**If the ant brings forth her eggs, it presages
rain. Glow-worm beetles appear.
Elderflower now in bloom.**

'In May and June come Pinks of all sorts,
specially the Blush-Pink; Roses of all kinds,
except the Musk, which comes later;
Honeysuckles, Strawberries, Bugloss,
Columbine, the French Marygold, Flos
Africanus, Cherry-tree in fruit, Ribes, Figs
in fruit, Rasps, Vine-flowers, Lavender in
flowers, the sweet Satyrian, with the white
flower; Herba Muscaria, Lilium, Convallium,
the Apple-tree in blossom.'
Francis Bacon *Of Gardens* 1625

JUNE

comes from *Juvenas*, it being dedicated to the Youth
of Rome. Ovid pretends that *Juno* gave it this Name.
Temperature: 58.9° Fahrenheit (14.9° Celsius).
Rainfall: 2 inches (5 cm).

Yellow Rose, *Rosa lutea*

Rosarians are now looking anxiously forward to receiving their due reward – abundance of roses in return for the many months of labour bestowed on the culture of the trees.

'No Wilderness – can be
Where this attendeth me –
No Desert Noon –
No fear of frost to come
Haunt the perennial bloom –
But Certain June!'
Emily Dickinson 1860

1

Common Scarlet Pimpernel, *Anagallis arvensis*

The hedges are now beginning to be in their highest beauty and fragrance. The place of the hawthorn is supplied by the flowers of the dog rose, the different hues of which, from a light blush to a deep crimson, form a most elegant variety of colour.

'This is one of the months in which the gardener is reaping the harvest of his previous month's labours most bounteously. Not that those labours are now to be relaxed, nor do I mean to allow that the good gardener finds any one month without its appropriate produce.'
George W. Johnson *The Gardener's Almanack for 1844*

2

3

Rose de Meaux, *Rosa provincialis*

Be sure not to cut grass in which daffodils are planted until the leaves are withered. It is usually safe to do it now.

'To grow roses well you must have shelter from cutting east winds, and if the position is not sheltered it must be made so by means of a wall, a fence of yew, borders of evergreens, or some other plan that will enhance rather then mar the beauty of the scene. Then there must be good drainage to carry off excess of moisture.'
Shirley Hibberd *Rustic Adornments for Homes of Taste* 1856

4

Indian Pink, *Dianthus chinensis*

Now, and even a little earlier, is the great pruning-time of the year for all spring-flowering shrubs. Common blue butterfly appears.

'See how the flowers, as at parade,
Under their colours stand display'd:
Each regiment in order grows,
That of the tulip, pink and rose.'
Andrew Marvell 1621–78 *Upon Appleton House*

Three-leafed China Rose, *Rosa sinica*

5

The early part of June is the best time to disbud carnations, which make far more buds than they can bring to perfection.

'Where I find her not, beauties vanish;
Whither I follow her, beauties flee;
Is there no method to tell her in Spanish
June's twice June since she breathed it with me?
Come, bud, show me the least of her traces,
Treasure my lady's lightest footfall!
– Ah, you may flout and turn up your faces –
Roses, you are not so fair after all!'
Robert Browning *Garden Fancies: The Flower's Name*
1844

Common Pink, *Dianthus deltoides*

6

Gooseberries for puddings, tarts, and *groseille foulée*, vulgarly called fool, are now plentiful. Dog-roses blooming.

'Beware of eating Apples this moneth. Set no herbes, hedges, nor trees in June, July, or August: and have an eye unto Antes, Emits, and Snailes in your gardens.'
William Ram *Little Dodoen* 1606

'Gather herbs for drying of all sorts as are now in flower, and hang them up in a dry shady place where they may dry leisurely, which will render them better for any purpose, than if they were dried in the sun.'
Philip Miller *The Gardeners Kalendar* 1732

7

Red Centaury, *Chironia centaureum*

Cut no asparagus after the first week in this month, for it will impoverish the roots. Meadow brown butterfly appears.

'It is now not so very long since carpet-bedding went out of fashion with a roar of contemptuous execration; and for a short period we were all for a return to what we spoke of as "Nature", but what was merely wobbly anarchy reduced to a high art.'
E. A. Bowles *My Garden in Spring* 1914

'Nodding foxgloves (*Digitalis*), white and purple, the witches' thimbles of the Gaelic-speaking Celts, range themselves in long flowering spikes between the deep grass in the Wild Flower Garden and the lines of yews, bright in June's richest gold and green foliage.'
Lucy H. Soutar *Monthly Gleanings in a Scottish Garden* 1909

8

Moneywort, Herb Twopence, or Creeping Loosestrife, *Lysimachia numularia*

Maria Theresa Earle born in 1836; gardening writer who created a garden at her home in Cobham, Surrey.

'I suppose it is the same with everything in life that one really cares about, and you must not, any of you, be surprised if you have moments in your gardening life of such profound depression and disappointment that you will almost wish you had been content to leave everything alone and have no garden at all. This is especially the case in a district affected by smoke or wind, or in a very light soil.'
Mrs Earle *Pot-Pourri from a Surrey Garden* 1897

Barberry, Pipperidge Bush of England, *Berberis vulgaris*

9

The strawberry season is beginning. Deadly nightshade in flower.

'No fruit, vegetables, or flowers seem half so fine as those we have planted and cultivated ourselves. The actual labour required soon becomes pleasant; and, till it has been tried, no one can tell the delight we take in watching and waiting for the effects of the work of our hands.'
Henrietta Wilson *The Chronicles of a Garden* 1863

'In Sutherlandshire at the present day, when the new potatoes are dug up all the family must taste them, otherwise "the spirits in them take offence, and the potatoes would not keep".'
J. G. Frazer *The Golden Bough* 1890

Bright Yellow Iris, *Iris pseudo-acorus*

10

In the early part of June the flower which we count on above all for pleasure is the iris. Pinks may now be propagated by pipings. Rosebay willow-herb in flower.

'It would be rather a difficult matter to sum up all the social qualities of flowers. Do we not always feel welcome when, on entering a room, we find a display of flowers on the table? Where there are flowers about, does not the hostess appear glad, the children pleased, the very parrot garrulous, at our arrival; the whole scene and all the personages more hearty, homely, and beautiful, because of those bewitching roses, and brugmansias, and pavonias, and mignionette? Assuredly, of all simple domestic ornaments flowers must have the first place.'
Shirley Hibberd *Rustic Adornments for Homes of Taste* 1856

11

Midsummer Daisy, *Chrysanthemum leucanthemum*

What a time the humble-bees are having just now! All the flowers seem specially built for them.

'Of all the implements, those used in gardening have changed the least. The hoe, equipped with a shell, antler, or animal scapula before the development of bronze or wrought iron, is prehistoric. Wooden rakes were known to the earliest Egyptians. Spades, sickles, pruning knives, all are of extremely ancient origin.'
Eleanor Perenyi *Green Thoughts* 1981

12

White Dog-rose, *Rosa arvensis*

The moss rose flowers now plentifully and adds its beauties to the damask and other garden sorts of rose.

'Come buy my fine roses,
My myrtles and stocks,
My sweet-smelling blossoms
And close-growing box.

Here's my fine rosemary, sage and thyme,
Come buy my ground ivy,
Here feverfew, gilliflowers and rue,
Come buy my knotted marjoram, too!

Here's your sweet lavender,
Sixteen sprigs a penny,
Which you will find, my ladies,
Will smell as sweet as any.'
Old London Street Cries

Garden Ranunculus, *Ranunculus asiaticus*

13

Purple foxglove in blossom. 'Foxglove' comes from the Anglo-Saxon *foxes-gleow,* a musical instrument hung with bells of different sizes. Bladder campion in flower.

'June is the month of sweet scents. Philadelphus or syringa as it is generally called burdens the air with its heavy perfume. The dark red sweet-williams offer their homely and unsophisticated fragrance; that of the pansies, although less obvious, is intimate and refined. The viola, unlike the stocks, does not broadcast her scent over the whole garden; she withholds it, reserving her secret sweetness for those who seek it and not for the casual passer-by.'
Patience Strong *The Glory of the Garden* 1947

Sweet Basil, *Ocimum basilicum*

14

Search for earwigs among curled leaves. Honeysuckle in flower.

'Basils are either herbs, or undershrubs, generally of a sweet and powerful scent: they are chiefly natives of the East Indies, and in this climate require protection from frost. They are raised in a hot-bed, but should have as much air as possible in mild weather. They may stand abroad from May to the end of September, or of October, according as the weather is more or less mild at this season. They should be kept moderately moist. In the East this plant is used both in cookery and medicine, and the seeds are considered efficacious against the poison of serpents.'
Elizabeth Kent *Flora Domestica* 1823

15

Sensitive Plant, *Mimosa sensitiva*

Alice Margaret Coats born in 1905 in Birmingham; garden historian.

'To work in the garden is to be brought into contact with the elements of botany, geography, ecology, genetics, chemistry and entomology – not to mention ornithology, bacteriology and meteorology – and interest may develop in any of these directions. Add to this the infinite number of plants from which the gardener can select, and it is apparent that no lifetime is long enough in which to explore the resources of a few square yards of ground.'
Alice Coats *Flowers and Their Histories* 1956

16

Moss Rose, *Rosa muscosa*

William Paul born in 1822 in Cheshunt, Hertfordshire; nurseryman who specialized in roses; author of *The Rose Garden* 1848.

'A few years since, gardening was the recreation of the few – the opulent, the scholar, the man of leisure. Reared on a botanical basis, it was scientific rather than popular, and Collections of plants with Botanical names was the chief aim of the cultivator. In recent times, the art has undergone an entire change, and what was of old the pursuit of the few, has, in varied forms, become the recreation and delight of the many.'
William Paul *Villa Gardening* 1855

Yellow Monkey Flower, *Mimulus luteus*

Collecting seed on sunny summer days is a delightful occupation.

'We have found that a moderately sized plant of common groundsel produces about two thousand and three hundred seeds, that of a dandelion about two thousand and seven hundred, and that of the sow thistle about eleven thousand and two hundred. These are facts worth bearing in mind. Wage a constant war against all weeds.'
Robert Adamson *The Cottage Garden* 1856

17

Horned Poppy, *Chelidonium glaucium*

Take softwood cuttings. Spotted palmate and bee orchises in flower.

'And dream of London, small, and white, and clean,
The clear Thames bordered by its gardens green.'
William Morris *Earthly Paradise* 1870

'The structure of seed-pods is an interesting study, also the manner in which the pods burst open with explosive force when the seed is ripe. The Cytisus or Broom expels its seeds with the power and sound of a miniature pistol. This is the favourite method of distribution with the leguminosae; the pea-pods are split asunder, being virtually roasted by the hot rays of the sun.'
Samuel Graveson *My Villa Garden* 1915

18

THIS IS THE PICTURE OF THE OLD HOUSE BY THE THAMES TO WHICH THE PEOPLE OF THIS STORY WENT. HEREAFTER FOLLOWS THE BOOK IT-SELF WHICH IS CALLED NEWS FROM NOWHERE OR AN EPOCH OF REST & IS WRITTEN BY WILLIAM MORRIS.

19

La Julienne de Nuit, *Hesperis tristis*

Euan Hillhouse Methven Cox born in 1893 in Westward, Carse of Gowrie; gardening writer who created a garden at his home in Glendoick, Perthshire.

'Scotland was famed for its gardeners before the outside world knew that there was a garden in Scotland. Why this should have been has long been a puzzle. It was a problem that worried the worthy Switzer, was commented upon by Tobias Smollett, and caused trouble towards the end of the eighteenth century when English gardeners complained that Scotsmen were usurping their places.'
E. H. M. Cox *A History of Gardening in Scotland* 1935

20

Doubtful Poppy, *Papaver dubium*

By the 20th or 24th of this month you may expect the blossom of the vine to open and discover fruit.

'A piece of the white Poppy Shell, as large as a half Crown piece, being boiled in Milk or Wine, is a very good Quantity to be used, where Sleep is required; and if that has not the desired Effect, you may double the Quantity, but never more, lest the Consequence proves fatal to those that take the Decoction.'
Batty Langley *New Principles of Gardening* 1728

Viper's Bugloss, *Echium vulgare*

Summer solstice, the longest day of the year. When the dogwood flowers appear, frost will not again appear.

'Dr Tanner asked whether the First Commissioner of Works would consent to relax the regulation with regard to Kew-gardens so that people should be allowed to take their lunch into the gardens with them. Mr Cremer said that the proposal of the hon. member would be regarded as a great boon by the working classes.'
The Times 21 June 1887

21

Canterbury Bell, *Campanula medium*

Cancer: 22 June–23 July. Enchanter's nightshade begins flowering. The gift of a few flowers will make anyone your friend.

'When you see the advertisement of a flower-show, it would be prudent to provide yourself on the day with an umbrella.'
Comic Almanac 1835–1853

'Sweet Williams, Canterbury bells and the deliciously fragrant old garden pinks mingle their perfume, at eventide, with the wafted essence of new-mown grass.'
Herbert Cowley *The Garden Year* 1936

22

23

Ladies' Slipper, *Cypripedium calceolus*

Midsummer Eve. Corn cockle flowering. Fern-seed is popularly supposed to bloom like gold or fire on Midsummer Eve.

'Rose hips, a Poppy head, the satin of Honesty, the queer horned seed vessel of Love-in-a-Mist may be left where desired, but a safe general rule is to cut off dead blooms as often as you can find time for it; even so, there will be self-sown plants in many unexpected and often charming combinations.'
Helena Swanwick *The Small Town Garden* 1907

24

St John's Wort, *Hypericum pulchrum*

Midsummer Day. Wild strawberries ripe. June is the best month to propagate a fresh stock of perennials from seed.

'The marigold that goes to bed with the sun
And with him rises weeping; these are flowers
Of middle summer, and I think they are give
To men of middle age.'
William Shakespeare *The Winter's Tale* 1610

Sweet William, *Dianthus barbatus*

25

Don't forget to keep the watering-can busy on peas, cabbages, onions and leeks. Greater knapweed flowers.

'The Bearded Pink, or Sweet-William – French *oeillet de poète* – is a native of Germany. Gerarde mentions it as being, in his time, highly esteemed "to deck up gardens, the bosoms of the beautiful, garlands, and crowns for pleasure". The narrow-leaved kinds are called Sweet-Johns: the broad leaved, unspotted kinds are by some named Tolmeiners and London-tufts; and the small speckled kind, London-pride.'
Elizabeth Kent *Flora Domestica* 1823

Alpine Hairy Blue Sowthistle, *Sonchus caeruleus*

26

A shower at this time of year is generally welcome.

'Seed-pods. If these are to be saved, let them be watched and gathered as they approach the ripening season; but if the seed be not wanted every decaying flower should be removed before the seed-pods swell, for nothing so completely destroys the flowers of anything as allowing the pods of seed to swell instead of removing them. Let one patch of Sweet Peas be allowed to bloom, and not a flower to be cut, and let another have every flower cut off the instant it begins to fade; and those which are allowed to seed will be completely out of flower and full of seed-pods, while the other continues to grow and bloom for weeks afterwards. It is the same with all flowers.'
George Glenny *Hand-Book to the Flower Garden and Greenhouse* 1873

27

Perforated St John's Wort, *Hypericum perforatum*

Elder in flower. Grasshoppers abundant.

'St John's Wort. Probably no herb has had so many legends and superstitions attached to it as this. In the Middle Ages the herb was regarded as a sure preventive of evil arising from the malignity of witches or demons. Gerarde wrote: "A balsam prepared from it is a most pretious remedie for deep wounds and those that are through the bodie, or for any wounds made with a venomed weapon." For chronic catarrh, and indeed for practically any complaint affecting the throat and lungs, as well as for restriction of the urinary passages, the usual infusion should be prepared and taken freely in wineglassful doses. The same infusion is an old-fashioned rustic remedy for bed-wetting in children or aged people.'
Mary Thorne Quelch *Herbs for Daily Use* 1941

28

Cornflower or Bluebottle, *Centaurea cyanus*

Cut off all the dead flowers of lilac, azalea and other blossoming trees and shrubs.

'Bluebottle, Cornflower. The Bluebottle was at one time far more popular than the Bluebell, with its washes of azure and silver. Before the flood of exotics began to pour into the English garden, the Bluebottle was much cultivated. "It is sowen in gardens, which by cunning looking to, doth often times become of other colours, and some also double" (Gerard). We grow it still. But it is one thing to raise a little patch of Bluebottle or Cornflower, another to see it by the acre, as in French cornfields. Bluebottle used to be taken against plague, poison, wounds, fevers, inflammations.'
Geoffrey Grigson *The Englishman's Flora* 1955

Yellow Rattle, *Rhinanthus crist-galli*

The foxglove begins to blow.

29

'Fill up the border with common roses – the
old cabbage, the white, the damask – these old
friends used to grow and flower without all the
care the new favourites get; keep pretty large
clumps of Canterbury bells, columbines,
snapdragons, foxgloves, pinks, stove carnations
and pansies, and with a judicious mixture of
beds of annuals, the borders will be always gay
and full.'
Henrietta Wilson *The Chronicles of a Garden* 1864

Yellow Cistus, *Cistus helianthemum*

**Joseph Dalton Hooker born in 1817 in
Halesworth, Suffolk; plant collector and most
celebrated botanist of the nineteenth century;
Director of Kew Gardens 1865–85 and
President of the Royal Society 1873–78.**

30

'Our own medicines are very largely taken from
what we call the vegetable kingdom; but their
composition is concealed from the patient by the
mysteries of prescriptions and of foreign names.
A sick man thinks himself effectually tended,
if he chance to make out that his doses contain
Taraxacum, Belladonna, Aconite, Hyoscyamus,
or Arneca, or if he be refreshed with Ammonia;
but he smiles contemptuously at the herb
woman who administers dent de lion,
nightshade, wolfsbane, henbane, elecampane,
or who burns horn in the sick chamber.'
Oswald Cockayne *Leechdoms, Wortcunning, and
Starcraft of Early England* 1864

JULY

was so called by Mark Antony, from Julius Caesar's being born in this Month. It is also called Quintilis, or the 5th Month. Temperature: 62.2° Fahrenheit (16.8° Celsius). Rainfall: 2.56 inches (6.5 cm).

Agrimony, *Agrimonia Eupatoria*

1

A period of leisure has at length arrived for those engaged in gardening for recreation alone.

'Agrimony. During the months of June and July this pretty wayside flower can hardly fail to arrest our attention by its tapering spikes of yellow blossoms, which have a faint odour of lemon, or as some say of apricots, an odour becoming more powerful if they are bruised.'
Anne Pratt *The Flowering Plants and Ferns of Great Britain* 1855

'In July come Gilliflowers of all varieties, Musk-Roses, the Lime-tree in blossom, early Pears, and Plums in fruit, Genitings [early apples], Codlins.'
Francis Bacon *Of Gardens* 1625

White Lily, *Lilium candidum*

2

When you water, do it thoroughly. A liberal soaking once a week will do more good than a daily trickle which does not penetrate the lower soil and draws the roots to the surface.

'I consider no trouble too great, whether the garden be large or small, to grow the beautiful stately Madonna Lily (*Lilium candidum*). It requires very different treatment from other Lilies, and flourishes in rich, heavy soils in full sun, where many Lilies would fail.'
Mrs Earle *Pot-Pourri from a Surrey Garden* 1897

3

Common Mallow, *Malva sylvestris*

St Phocas, a gardener, 3rd century AD. Dog days, from 3 July to 11 August, are the hottest part of the year.

'Though the earwig is so common, till lately its history was only imperfectly understood; and even now many persons are not aware that it has wings carefully folded under its shining wing-cases, and also that it is the only insect which takes care of its young. All other insects die as soon as they have laid their eggs, but the earwig broods over its young as a hen does over her chickens, and collects them with great care when they are scattered about.'
Jane Loudon *The Amateur Gardener's Calendar* 1847

4

Tawny Day Lily of China, *Hemerocallis fulva*

The beginning of this month sow the last crop of kidney-beans, where they may be defended from morning frosts in autumn, for this crop will continue bearing till Michaelmas, provided they are not injured by frost.

'Elder is perhaps the most neglected hedgerow plant, though it is the source of elderflower wine, of cordial, and also of an excellent pudding – the flowers deep-fried in batter and sprinkled with sugar are a great delicacy. Elders keep witches at bay, and any old cottage garden that has not been modernized will have one growing alongside the house.'
Derek Jarman *Derek Jarman's Garden* 1995

Double Yellow Rose, *Rosa sulphurea*

5

Sweet peas in blossom. The largest rosebush on record is located in Tombstone, Arizona, according to the American Rose Society. The banksia rose was planted in 1885 and it now extends over 8000 square feet on a trellis at the Rose Tree Inn.

'Gather ye Rose-buds while ye may,
Old Time is still a flying:
And this same flower that smiles to day,
To morrow will be dying.'
Robert Herrick *To the Virgins, to make much of Time* 1648

Hawkweed or Purple-eyed Succory, *Crepis barbata*

6

Great bindweed flowering. Take semi-hardwood cuttings.

'Everywhere, during the fruit season, may be seen gangs of women and boys busily engaged in gathering Raspberries, Gooseberries, and Currants. Collectively, they earn large sums of money, good hands making as much as 11s. per day at Gooseberry picking, but the average rate is only about 6s. per day, and that only by means of hard work from light till dark.'
C. W. Shaw *The London Market Gardens* 1879

7

Nasturtium, *Tropaeolum majus*

The head of globe artichokes should be cut when about three parts open. Catmint and purple loosestrife in flower.

'There is scarce a Cottage in most of the Southern Parts of England but hath its proportionable Garden, so great a delight do most of men take in it; that they may not only please themselves with the view of the Flowers, Herbs, and Trees, as they grow, but furnish themselves and their Neighbours upon extraordinary occasions, as Nuptials, Feasts, and Funerals, with the proper products of their Gardens.'
John Worlidge *The Art of Gardening* 1677

8

Evening Primrose, *Oenothera biennis*

Always try to give away to those with no vegetable garden anything of which you have a superabundance.

'The common Evening Primrose is such a weed (the definition of a weed is a plant out of place), beautiful as it is, that people fight shy of the whole family of *Oenothera*, but this is a great mistake. *Oenothera Youngii* in a damp soil is one of the most beautiful yellow flowers and the red stalks show up the blossom in a wonderful way; the tufts are planted in October and divided every other year; it can also be grown from seed sown in July.'
Mrs Earle and Ethel Case *Gardening for the Ignorant* 1912

Tall Marsh Sowthistle, *Sonchus palustri*

Hornbeam, beech, quick and privet hedges should be cut. Harebell begins flowering.

9

'July-flowers of the Wall, or Wall July-flowers, Wall-flowers, or Bee-flowers, or Winter-July-flowers, because growing in the walls even in winter, and good for Bees, will grow even in stone-walls, they will seem dead in Summer and yet revive in Winter they yield seed plentifully, which you may sow at any time, or in broken earth, especially on the top of a mud-wall, but moist.'
William Lawson *The Country House-wifes Garden* 1617

Speckled Snapdragon, *Antirrhinum triphyllum*

This is the best month, particularly the early part of it, to strike myrtles.

10

'Columella alludes to this flower as "the stern and furious lion's gaping mouth". Its English names are Snap Dragon, Lion's Snap, Toad's Mouth, Dog's Mouth, and Calf's Snout. In many rural districts the Snap Dragon is believed to possess supernatural powers, and to be able to destroy charms. It was formerly supposed that when suspended about the person, this plant was a protection from witchcraft, and that it caused a maiden so wearing it to appear "gracious in the sight of people".'
Richard Folkard *Plant Lore, Legends and Lyrics* 1884

11

Yellow Lupin, *Lupinus floevus*

The tops and side-shoots of tomatoes must be pinched out. White admiral butterflies emerge. Marjoram now in flower. The oldest seed in the world is believed to be the arctic lupin, which germinated in 1966 and, according to radiocarbon tests, dates back 10,000 to 15,000 years.

'Lupins make a riot of colour in pink, blue, white, yellow, salmon, and apricot, with an indescribable array of intermediate so-called art shades.'
Herbert Cowley *The Garden Year* 1936

'The Horticultural Society of Seven Dials has been presented, by the Society of Antiquaries, with the identical pumpkin converted by the fairy into Cinderella's chariot.'
George Cruikshank *Comic Almanack 1835*

12

Great Snapdragon, *Antirrhinum purpureum*

Strawberries of all sorts now begin to be plentiful. Marbled white butterflies appear.

'There's never a garden in all the parish but what there's endless waste in it for want o' somebody as could use everything up. It's what I think to myself sometimes, as there need nobody run short o' victuals if the land was made the most on, and there was never a morsel but what could find its way to a mouth. It sets one thinking o' that – gardening does.'
George Eliot *Silas Marner* 1861

Blue Lupin, *Lupinus hirsutus*

**John Clare born in 1793 in Helpston,
Northamptonshire; under-gardener and poet.**

13

'And where the marjoram once, and sage, and rue,
And balm, and mint, with curled-leaf parsley grew,
And double marygolds, and silver thyme,
And pumpkins neath the window used to climb;
And where I often when a child for hours
Tried through the pales to get the tempting flowers,
As lady's laces, everlasting peas,
True-love-lies-bleeding, with the hearts-at-ease,
And golden rods, and tansy running high
That o'er the pale-tops smiled on passers-by;
Flowers in my time that every one would praise,
Though thrown like weeds from gardens nowadays.'
John Clare 1793–1864 *The Cross Roads*

Red Lupin, *Lupinus perennis*

**Garden tiger-moth appears. Humming-bird
hawk-moth visits geranium and clematis
flowers.**

14

'An American visitor, very proud of her own
garden, asked her English host why she took
the trouble to grow so common and so
commonplace a wild plant as the lupin. So a
visitor from the Argentine might ask why we
grow zinnias or a Newfoundlander wonder at
the presence of golden rod, one of the worst
native weeds, in our beds.'
William Beach Thomas *In Praise of Flowers* 1948

'Against mental vacancy and against folly; put
into ale bishopwort, lupins, betony, the
southern or Italian fennel, nepte, water
agrimony, cockle, marche, then let the man
drink.'
Leech Book of Bald 10th Century

15

Small Cape, Purple and White Marigold, *Calendula pluvialis*

William Robinson born in 1838 in County Down, Ireland; pioneer of natural gardening and friend of Gertrude Jekyll; created a garden at Gravetye, East Grinstead; author of *The Wild Garden* 1870.

'There is no such thing as a style fitted for every situation; only one who knows and studies the ground well will ever make the best of a garden, and any "style" may be right where the site fits it.'
William Robinson *The English Flower Garden* 1883

'In this month is St Swithin's Day,
On which, if it rain, they say
Full forty days after it will
Or more, or less, some rain distil.'
Poor Robin's Almanac 1697

16

Convolvulus, *Convolvulus purpureus*

About the middle of this month you should sow spinach for winter use. Traveller's joy in flower.

'Vegetable: organic body endowed with life and deprived of feeling. They will not let me off with that definition, I know. People want minerals to live, vegetables to feel, and even formless matter to be imbued with feeling. Although that may be so according to modern physics, I have never been able, nor will I ever be able to express the ideas of other people, when these ideas do not coincide with mine. I have often seen a dead tree which I previously saw alive, but the death of a stone is an idea which would never enter my head. I see delicate feeling in my dog, but I have never noticed any in a cabbage.'
Jean-Jacques Rousseau 1712–78 *Notes Towards a Dictionary of Botanical Terms*

Sweet Pea, *Lathyrus odoratus*

Purple lavender in flower. Sweet peas require the constant picking of pods, if the flowering is to be continuous.

'Here are sweet peas, on tip-toe for a flight:
With wings of gentle flush o'er delicate white,
And taper fingers catching at all things,
To bind them all about with tiny rings.'
John Keats *I stood tip-toe upon a little hill* 1817

17

Autumn Marigold, *Chrysanthemum coronarium*

Gilbert White born in 1720 in Selborne, Hampshire; naturalist.

'The sun, at noon, looked as blank as a clouded moon, and shed a rust-coloured ferruginous light on the ground, and floors of rooms; but was particularly lurid and blood-coloured at rising and setting. All the time the heat was so intense that butcher's meat could hardly be eaten on the day after it was killed; and the flies swarmed so in the lanes and hedges that they rendered the horses half frantic, and riding irksome. The country people began to look with a superstitious awe at the red, louring aspect of the sun; and indeed there was reason for the most enlightened person to be apprehensive; for, all the while, Calabria and part of the isle of Sicily were torn and convulsed with earthquakes; and about that juncture a volcano sprung out of the sea on the coast of Norway.'
Gilbert White *The Natural History of Selborne* 1789

18

19

Golden Hawkweed, *Hieracium auranticum*

An abundance of tepid water should be given to marrows.

'Friends, books, a garden, and perhaps his pen,
Delightful industry enjoy'd at home,
And Nature, in her cultivated trim
Dress'd to his taste, inviting him abroad –
Can he want occupation who has these?'
William Cowper 1731–1800 *The Task*

20

Virginian Dragon's Head, *Dracocephalus virginianum*

Onions should be ready to pull and dry in the sun.

'Some annuals look well even as single plants, branching out and flowering in an independent free way, quite as handsomely as some biennials. Clarkia pulchella, blue and yellow lupines, purple candytuft, and the large everlastings, seem to like occasionally thus to be left alone in their glory.'
Henrietta Wilson *The Chronicles of a Garden* 1864

Philadelphian Lily, *Lilium philadelphicum*

In thirsty July would the parched earth be glad of a moistening shower to refresh and revive the scorched vegetable.

21

'I know a little garden close
Set thick with lily and red rose
Where I would wander if I might
From dewy dawn to dewy night,
And have one with me wandering.'
William Morris *The Life and Death of Jason* 1867

African Lily, *Agapanthus umbellatus*

Climbing plants must be attended to every two or three days, that the growing shoots may be trained to their proper places.

22

'I have a garden plot,
Wherein there wants nor hearbs, nor roots,
    nor flowers;
Flowers to smell, roots to eate, hearbs, for
    the pot,
And dainty shelters when the welkin lowers:
Sweet-smelling beds of lillies, and of roses,
Which rosemary banks and lavender
    incloses.'
Richard Barnfield *The Affectionate Shepherd* 1594

23

Musk-flower, *Scabious-atro purpurea*

The sunflower begins to blow. Ring doves congregate.

'It is not the least Glory of a Garden of Pleasure to be stored with variety of flowers, as to present somewhat of Beauty for every Month in the year. To obtain this, the readiest and most natural way is, to make a collection of such Flowers as will be in actual Flowering of their own Nature every Month in the Year: For there are some flowers as natural to December, as others are to May, or June, or July.'
Robert Sharrock *An Improvement to the Art of Gardening* 1694

24

Lupin Tree, *Lupinus arboreus*

Leo: 24 July–22 August. Thinking time is a most necessary part of gardening work, though not always easy.

'In dry weather observe to water all such plants as have been lately transplanted, and be sure always to do this in an evening, for one watering at that time is of more service than three at any other time of the day, the moisture having time to penetrate the ground (and reach to the extream fibres of the root, by which they receive their nourishment) before the sun appears to exhale it; whereas when it is given in a morning, the sun coming on soon after, the moisture is drawn up before it reaches the root.'
Philip Miller *The Gardeners Kalendar* 1732

Pure White Herb Christopher, *Actaea spicata*

25

All sorts of herbs for the kitchen are very good, if the gardener has minded from time to time to cut them down for shooting afresh. On 25 July 1979, it rained for 24 hours for a US precipitation record of 43 inches in Alvin, Texas.

'And thus have we presented you a Taste of our English Garden Housewifry in the matter of Sallets; And though some of them may be Vulgar, (as are most of the best things); Yet she was willing to impart them to shew the Plenty, Riches and Variety of the Sallet-Garden; And to justifie what has been asserted of the Possibility of living (not unhappily) on Herbs, and Plants, according to Original and Divine Institution, improved by Time and long Experience.'
John Evelyn *A Discourse of Salletts* 1699

Field Chamomile or Corn Feverfew, *Matricaria chamomilla*

26

A good supply of soft water is very useful during summer. Pour tea and leaves on your azaleas, rhododendrons, or camellias.

'It is possible that birds do some destruction out of pure mischief, but sometimes they attack tender juicy roots and fruit because they have no other means of quenching their thirst. A regular supply of water should be provided, preferably in the form of a bowl or dish with shallow sloping sides, deeper towards the centre and raised above the ground to give the birds a reasonable security from cats.'
V. N. Solly *Gardens for Town and Suburb* 1926

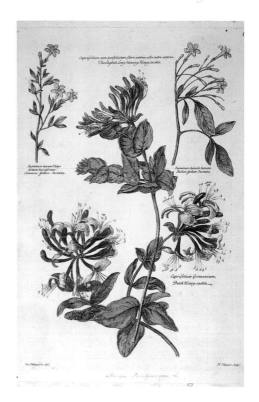

27

Purple Loosestrife, *Lythrum salicaria*

Persons at this time of year should caution children against eating the berries of the deadly nightshade, several fatal accidents have occurred from their being devoured unthinkingly.

'The honeysuckle's clinging sweets
Vie with the blushing rose;
And nature's flowers spring forth in heaps,
To deck the wild hedge rows.
O beautiful but hot July,
What treasures do you bring
I'd chant, another hour, your praise,
But am too hot to sing!'
Pictorial Almanac 1848

Mountain Groundsel, *Senecio montanus*

28

Geranium cuttings will now strike like weeds in the open ground, from which they are easily potted. Feverfew now in flower.

'Our England is a garden, and such gardens are
    not made
By singing: "Oh, how beautiful!" and sitting in
    the shade,
While better men than we go out and start their
    working lives
At grubbing weeds from gravel-paths with
    broken dinner-knives.'
Rudyard Kipling *The Glory of the Garden* 1911

Red Chironia, *Chironia centaurium*

29

The most effectual method of catching wasps is by touching them with twigs besmeared with bird-lime.

'Wasps fix upon the finest fruit, and, in some seasons, long before it is ripe. They will eat a greengage plum to a shell; and, while they spoil your fruit, they will not scruple to sting you if you come to interrupt their enjoyment.'
William Cobbett *The English Gardener* 1829

'Seeds of hardy things cannot be sown too soon after they are ripe. Nothing exhibits more healthy growth than a self-sown seedling; and if it be so, how can we do better than sow directly the seed is ripe and gathered?'
George Glenny *The Handbook to the Flower Garden and Greenhouse* 1873

30

White Mullein, *Verbascum lychnitis*

Alicia Amherst born in 1865 in Poole, Dorset; plant collector and garden historian.

'There is much more than meets the eye in English Gardens. Even the most insignificant have their story to tell, for every stage of English history is reflected in them. They have gradually changed through the centuries, and each phase of our political development, our foreign policy, our wars, and our discoveries has left its mark on our gardens.'
Alicia Amherst *The History of Gardening* 1895

'July-flowers, commonly called Gillyflowers, or Clove July-flowers, (I call them so, because they flower in July) they have the name of Cloves, of the sent. I may well call them the King of flowers except the Rose, & the best sort of them are called Queen-July-flowers. I have of them nine or ten several colours, & divers of them as big as Roses; of all the flowers (save the Damask Rose) they are the most pleasant to sight and smell.'
William Lawson *The Country House-wifes Garden* 1617

31

Primrose-leafed Yellow Mullein, *Verbascum virgatum*

See that your roses are dead-headed to ensure a good second crop of flowers. Small skipper butterfly appears.

'July and August are cruel months in most of these United States. Heat and drought and insects must daily be combated, while plants which made the picture glorious in the early months are preparing underground to do it again next year.'
Mrs C. H. Stout, New Jersey 1938 (*Our Garden Heritage*, ed. Alice Sloane Anderson 1961)

AUGUST

was thus called, on account of the Actions of
Augustus Caesar, which happened in this Month.
Temperature: 61.3° Fahrenheit (16.3° Celsius).
Rainfall: 2.43 inches (6 cm).

1

Stramony or Thorn-apple, *Datura stramonium*

**Lammas Day. The term Lammas Day is
a corruption of Loafmass, and is a remnant of
a very ancient British custom of celebrating
the gift of Ceres, or the frumentous produce
of the earth; whence bread is made, and
human life supported.**

'In August come Plums of all sorts in fruit,
Pears, Apricots, Barberries, Filberts, Musk-
Melons, Monks-hoods, of all colours.'
Francis Bacon *Of Gardens* 1625

'Now cabbage, apples, pears, and plumbs,
Full ripe and good, this season comes;
But don't with them too merry make,
For fear they make your belly ach.'
Poor Sir Robin 1790

2

Tiger Lily, *Lilium tigrum*

**Rosemary, the grace of herbs here in
England, in other countries common.
To set slips immediately after Lammas
is the surest way.**

'Destroy thistles, which, some say may be done
by letting them grow till they are in full bloom
and then cutting them with a scythe about an
inch from the surface of the ground. The stem
being hollow the rain water and dews descend
into the heart of the plant, and it soon dies.'
Thomas Green Fessenden *The New England
Farmer's Almanack for 1828*

Hollyhock, *Althea rosea*

3

A good housewife may, and will, gather store of herbs for the pot about Lammas, and dry them, and pound them, and in winter they will do good service.

'Ambition. The emblem of that crime by which Wolsey tells us the angels fell is the tall and stately *Hollyhock*. A few years ago it was often designated the "garden mallow", and, indeed, belongs to the mallow family. From the fact that it is known in France as *Rose d'outre Mer*, or "rose from beyond the sea", it has been surmised that it was first introduced into Europe from Syria by the Crusaders. The blossom of the Hollyhock is said to furnish a great quantity of bee honey.'
The Language of Flowers 19th Century

Bluebells, *Campanula rotundifolia*

4

John Tradescant born in 1608 in Meopham, Kent; son of John Tradescant (c. 1570–1638), who gave his name to Tradescantia; collected plants in Virginia; gardener to Charles I; buried in the garden of the Museum of Garden History, Lambeth Palace Road, London.

'At this time many people take their annual holiday, and it is well before leaving home to go round the garden, and, as far as possible, to take all precautions against things getting out of order in one's absence. For this purpose a final staking should be given to such plants as have outgrown their supports, and a thorough clearance made of all young weeds which may flourish unchecked when the hoe is idle.'
The Amateur Gardener's Diary and Dictionary 1904

5

Egyptian Water Lily, *Nelumbo nilotica*

The blackcurrant contains more than four times as much vitamin C as the orange. Poplar hawk-moth appears.

'If you shall have any of these Flowers stolen, and if you would be revenged on the party, or would put a jest or a jeer, you shall accomplish your desire thus; take an Elecompane root dry and beaten to powder, then sprinkle it upon your Gilliflowers, or put it into the midst, then give your Flowers to the party that you desire to be revenged of, let it be a he or she they will delight in smelling to it, then they will draw this powder into their nostrils which will make them fall a sneezing, and a great trouble to the eyes, and by your leave will make the tears run down their thighs.'
Stephen Blake *The Compleat Gardeners Practice* 1664

6

Colchicum variegatum.

Meadow Saffron, *Colchicum autumnalis*

Lavender is still in full flower and the cutting it to scent linen ought to be no longer delayed.

'The Colchicums or Meadows Saffron, so termed, being first taken out of the Meadows, these Flowers are called Naked Boyes because they appear naked out of the Earth and are withered and gone before the green leaves appear.'
John Worlidge *The Art of Gardening* 1677

'Who does not love the faint odor of lavender on the cool bed linen, and have not many of us some childhood recollection of sage? My nurse, I now believe, thought it a perfect panacea. If we tumbled in the brook or ate green apples, a cup of hot sage tea was administered.'
Helena Rutherfurd Ely *Another Hardy Garden Book* 1905

Common Amaranth, *Amaranthus hypochondriacus*

7

As soon as raspberries have fruited, cut out the old canes. Silver-washed fritillary butterflies appear. Mustard plants now beginning to seed.

'Most poetical of all flowers in meaning is the *Amaranth*. It has been selected as the symbol of *immortality*, and has ever been associated with Death as the portal through which the soul must pass to Eternity. These flowers if gathered and dried will long preserve their beauty.'
The Language of Flowers 19th Century

'In the heat of sommer, what place is fitter for the table, than some sweet, shady, coole Arbour in the Garden? And what meats better befitting that time of the yeare, than some dainty dishes made of the coole fruits of the Orchard?'
Ralph Austen *A Treatise of Fruit-Trees* 1653

Love Lies-a-bleeding, *Amaranthus procumbens*

8

A public meeting was held in 1844 Manchester Town Hall, chaired by the Mayor, to raise subscriptions for public parks. A total of £7000 was raised.

'I mind me in the days departed,
How often underneath the sun
With childish bounds I used to run
To a garden long deserted.

Old garden rose-trees hedged it in,
Bedropt with roses waxen-white
Well satisfied with dew and light
And careless to be seen.

Long years ago it might befall,
When all the garden flowers were trim,
The grave old gardener prided him
On these the most of all.'
Elizabeth Barrett Browning *The Deserted Garden* 1838

9

Yellow Jacobean Ragwort, *Senecio jacobea*

Eleanour Sinclair Rohde born in 1881 in Allepy, Travancore; gardening writer who repopularized the cultivation of herbs; author of *The Story of the Garden* 1932.

'The very word "herb-garden" suggests old world peace and fragrance. It conjures up a vision, as remote and yet as familiar as memory, of a secluded pleasaunce full of sunlight and delicious scents and radiant with the colours and quiet charm of all the lovable old-fashioned plants one so rarely sees nowadays. From Saxon days until the end of the eighteenth century the herb-garden reigned supreme in England, and now that we are reviving so much that is old and pleasant, perhaps we shall be wise enough to restore the herb-garden with its beautiful colours and its fragrance to its former pride of place.'
Eleanour Sinclair Rohde *The Scented Garden* 1931

10

Balsam, *Impatiens balsamea*

Take root cuttings of perennial flowers. Devil's scabious and purple loosestrife in flower.

'For it is not to be doubted; but as God hath given man things profitable: so hath he allowed him honest comfort, delight and recreation in all the works of his hands. Nay, all his labours under the Sunne without this are troubles, and vexation of minde: for what is greedy gaine without delight? but moyling, and turmoyling in slavery? But comfortable delight, with content, is the good of everything, and the patterne of heaven. And who can deny, but the principall end of an Orchard is the honest delight of one wearied with the worke of his lawful calling? The very works of, and in an Orchard and Garden, are better than the ease and rest of and from other labours.'
William Lawson *A New Orchard and Garden* 1618

China Aster, *Aster chinensis*

11

Moles become very injurious to the farmer and gardener at this time of year by burrowing underground and destroying the roots in the earth.

'One of the most delightful things about gardening is the freemasonry it gives with other gardeners, and the interest and pleasure all gardeners get by visiting other people's gardens. We all have a lot to learn and in every new garden there is a chance of finding inspiration – new flowers, different arrangement or fresh treatment for old subjects. Even if it is a garden you know by heart there are twelve months in the year and every month means a different garden, and the discovery of things unexpected all the rest of the year.'
Margery Fish *We Made a Garden* 1956

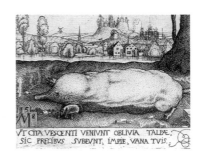

Great Corn Sowthistle, *Sonchus avensis*

12

The long hot summer of 1911 is recorded by several gardening writers:

'In the drought of 1911 a splendid bed of phloxes was kept going by making some holes with a crowbar, three round each clump, and pouring water down the holes, and then mulching lightly with peat moss. Phloxes are the first to suffer from dry weather, but these kept their freshness and beauty when all else was dried up in the other borders.'
Alice Martineau *The Herbaceous Garden* 1913

'The only bright spots in my parched garden in the tropical heat of 1911 were half a dozen outdoor tomatoes, which in those days were only beginning to be recognised as an essential foodstuff. In south Dorset the sun blazed all day in a Mediterranean sky of brass from the middle of May until the middle of September.'
Claude Scudamore Jarvis *Gardener's Medley* 1951

13

Marsh Groundsel, Great Fen Rag-wort or Bird's Tongue, *Senecio paludosis*

August 1995 was the hottest in the UK since temperature records began in the late 1600s. Sunshine totals were a record 55 per cent above the normal for the country as a whole, the sunniest August since detailed sunshine records began at the end of the nineteenth century.

'Ev'n in the stifling bosom of the town,
A garden in which nothing thrives, has charms
That sooth the rich possessor.'
William Cowper *The Task* 1785

14

Elegant Zinnia, *Zinnia elegans*

Pick up fruit drops. Autumnal hawk-bit in flower. Take cuttings of mint, sage, winter savory and thyme.

'About the fourteenth of this month, you may sow early Yorkshire and Battersea Cabbage seeds; for what you sow earlier, will run to seed in the Spring, if the Winter is mild; and what you sow later, will not have strength enough to resist the cold; and though they stand out the Winter, they will not come so early as you could wish.'
James Justice *The Gardener's New Kalendar* 1767

White Virgin's Bower, *Clematis vitalba*

15

Lavender hedges may now be trimmed. Wasp nests abundant.

'The beautiful race of Clematises deserves a volume to itself. The different species bloom from March to December, and every shade of colour, from white to blue, from yellow to scarlet, is represented. In the matter of scent, too, few flowers possess a sweeter fragrance than Clematis flammula, the wild Clematis of Southern Europe. This species and the hedge Clematis (C. vitalba), or Traveller's Joy of our English hedges, are the two best known species, and, until some forty years ago, were, with C. viticella, almost the only kinds grown. About that time, however, the Japanese and Chinese species were introduced and English gardeners were made familiar with the azurea, patens, montana, and lanuginosa species.'
Harry Roberts *The Chronicle of a Cornish Garden* 1901

Belladonna Lily, *Amaryllis belladonna*

16

Mulberries ripe.

'Gather fruites, and flowers, as neere as you can to the time of the full Moone; for then have they most vertue, being then most full of juyce.'
Thomas Lakes *The Countrey-Mans Kalender* 1627

'If you merely wish to be reminded of the routine culture, and require also to see that it is done, the calendar in the almanac may do; but for private use, make a calendar of your own, and don't forget to read it now and then.'
Henrietta Wilson *The Chronicles of a Garden* 1864

17

Toad-flax Snapdragon, *Antirrhinum linaria*

Bats now begin to be seen again of an evening and sometimes enter our apartments and conceal themselves in the furniture.

'Records of changes made in the garden, a walk altered, a tree taken out, or one planted, a plot laid down in grass, or a new border made, – all of these, if duly recorded in a garden-book, become matters of interest in after years, all the more when those who then wrought by our side are removed from us by distance or by death, recalling, as they do, happy hours passed away.'
Henrietta Wilson *The Chronicles of a Garden* 1864

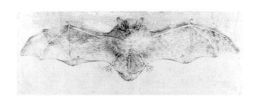

18

Marigold, *Tagetes erecta*

August is a good month to make a strawberry bed. Small copper butterfly appears.

'I cannot lay too great stress upon the neatness in which a lady's garden should be kept. If it is not beautifully neat, it is nothing. For this reason, keep every plant distinct in the flower-beds; let every tall flower be well staked, that the wind may not blow it prostrate; rake away dead leaves from the beds, and trim every flower-root from discoloured leaves, weeds, &c; remove all weeds and stones the moment they appear, and clear away decaying stems, which are so littering and offensive to the eye. There is always some employment of this kind for every week in the year.'
Louisa Johnson *Every Lady Her Own Flower Gardener* 1839

Timothy or Common Cat's Tail Grass, *Phleum panniculatum* or *P. asperum*

19

Jane Wells Loudon born in 1807 in Birmingham; horticultural writer; founded and edited the *Ladies Magazine of Gardening* in 1842.

'A lady, with a small light spade may, by repeatedly digging over the same line, and taking out only a little earth at a time, succeed in doing all the digging that can be required in a small garden; and she will not only have the satisfaction of seeing the garden created, as it were, by her own hands, but she will find her health and spirits wonderfully improved by the exercise, and by the reviving smell of the fresh earth.'
Jane Loudon *Gardening for Ladies* 1840

Dandelion, *Leontodon serotinus*

20

You can cultivate dandelions until they are larger than marigolds and the young leaves make an excellent salad. Mistle thrushes congregate.

'Blanched Dandelion leaves, Dandelion wine in the cottages, Dandelion beer for steel workers – these are all relics of the plant in medicine. It is diuretic and cleansing, still "piss-a-bed" up and down the country, though the name has been politely ignored (unlike the French *pissenlit*). You tell the time, and foretell the future, by blowing on the seed-head.'
Geoffrey Grigson *The Englishman's Flora* 1955

21

French Marigold, *Tagetes patula*

This is a good month in which to strike cuttings. Sweet peas require ample water and doses of liquid manure.

'Good tilth bring seedes,
ill tilture weedes.

Yong plants sone die,
that growe to drie.'
Thomas Tusser *Five Hundreth Points of Good Husbandry* 1573

22

Timothy or Common Cat's Tail Grass, *Phleum pratense*

Opening of Queen's Park and Philips Park in 1846 in Manchester and Peel Park in Salford. They were free of charge and open every day of the week.

'The Earth now yields to the patient Husbandman the fruits of his labours. This Month returns the Countrymans expences into his Coffers with increase, and encourages him to another years adventure. If this Month prove dry, warm, and free from high winds, it rejoyceth the Countrymans heart, encreaseth his gains, and abates a great part of his Disbursements.'
John Worlidge *Kalendarium Rusticum* 1675

Common Tansy, *Tanacetum vulgare*

**Virgo: 23 August–23 September. Starlings
assemble in large flocks. The marvel of Peru
flowers. This plant is called the four o'clock
flower from its period of opening in the
afternoon.**

23

'Another World was search'd, through Oceans
    new,
To find the Marvel of Peru.'
Andrew Marvell 1621–78 *The Mower Against Gardens*

'*Mirabilis jalapa*, Marvel of Peru. We have not
as yet any instructions from the people of India,
concerning the nature or vertues of this plant:
the which is esteemed as yet for his rarenesse,
beautie, and sweetness of his floures, than for
any vertues knowne; but it is a pleasant plant
to decke the gardens of the curious.'
John Gerard *Herball 1597*

Tall Sunflower, *Helianthus annuus*

**Carry wood or other fuel home before the
winter. Winged ants migrate. The marigold
was known in Wiltshire as the Measle-flower
because of its use as a tea to cure measles.**

24

'The sunflower was one of the earliest
introductions from the New World, and was
grown in Europe before 1569. Gerard boasted
that in his Holborn garden it grew to a height
of fourteen feet and bore a flower weighing
three pounds and two ounces; but this was
easily surpassed by de Passe, who says that
at Madrid it grew to twenty-four feet and at
Padua to forty feet.'
Alice Coats *The Book of Flowers* 1973

25

Perennial Sunflower, *Helianthus multiflorus*

Take cuttings of ceanothus, cotoneaster, escallonia and hypericum.

'Where rustic taste at leisure trimly weaves
The rose and straggling woodbine to the eaves,
And on the crowded spot that pales enclose
The white and scarlet daisy rears in rows –
Training the trailing peas in bunches neat,
Perfuming evening with a luscious sweet –
And sun-flowers planting for their gilded show,
That scale the window's lattice ere they blow,
And sweet to habitants within the sheds,
Peep through the diamond pane their golden heads.'
John Clare *Rural Evening* 1821

Banded Amaryllis, *Amaryllis vittata*

**Hollyhocks may be propagated by cuttings.
Bees and wasps kill the drones.**

26

'Beans be damned by Pythagoras' sentence, for
it is said, that by oft use thereof, the wits are
dulled and cause many dreams.'
Bartholomew Anglicus *The Properties of Things* 1470

'August. Sleepe but a little. Live very well, but
lust very little.'
Daniel Browne *A New Almanack and Prognostication*
1620

Hedge Hawkweed, *Hieracium umbellatum*

**By far the most important flowers of the
month are the autumn-flowering phloxes,
about the most valuable of the many floral
beauties which North America has given us.**

27

'A few simple borders, well stocked with mixed
herbaceous plants, such as primulas, paeonies,
lilies, phloxes, hollyhocks, and
carnations, would, in many instances,
afford more real pleasure and ever-
changing interest than the most
gorgeous display of bedding plants hemmed
in between two glaring walls, or exposed on
a·great treeless, turfless place like the blazing fire
at the mouth of a coal-pit.'
Shirley Hibberd *The Amateur's Flower Garden* 1871

'It was observed at the end of August, 1742,
great damage was done to the pastures in the
country, particularly about Bristol by swarms
of grasshoppers; and the like happened in the
same year at Pennsylvania to a surprising degree.'
William Hone *The Every-Day Book* 1830

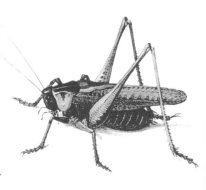

28

Golden Rod, *Solidago virga aurea*

Joshua Major born in 1786 in Owston near Doncaster, Yorkshire; nurseryman who designed the first urban public parks in Manchester 1846.

'I would, by no means, allow the indecent practice of open bathing in these waters; provision ought to be made for that purpose elsewhere.'
Joshua Major *The Theory and Practice of Landscape Gardening* 1852

'Raw fruit though ripe may sicknesse bring,
Unripe much eaten, a dangerous thing:
If now a Surfet thou dost take,
When others sleep, then thou must wake.'
John Neve *A New Almanack* 1611

29

Yellow Hollyhock, *Althea flava*

John Locke born in 1632 in Wrington, Somerset; philosopher.

'A vineyard from its planting will last fifty, eighty, or an hundred years. The older the vineyard the fewer the grapes, but the better the wine. I have been told that a sheep's horn buried at the root of a vine will make it bear well even in barren ground. I have no great faith in it, but mention it because it may so easily be tried.'
John Locke *Observations Upon the Growth and Culture of Vines and Olives* 1766

Guernsey Lily, *Amaryllis sarniensis*

30

Feast day of the patron of gardeners, St Fiacre, an Irish monk who died in 670. Bulls begin to make that remarkable shrill noise which is peculiar to autumn.

'The Guernsey Lily is a native of Japan. When in full beauty, it has the appearance of a fine gold tissue wrought on a rose-coloured ground; and when it begins to fade, it is pink. If beheld in full sunshine, it seems studded with diamonds; but by candle-light, looks rather as if it were spangled with fine gold-dust. When the flower begins to wither, the petals assume a deep crimson colour. The flowers begin to appear towards the end of August, and the head is usually three weeks gradually expanding. This plant is said to have been taken to Guernsey by a vessel wrecked there on its return from Japan.'
Elizabeth Kent *Flora Domestica* 1823

Pheasant's-eye, *Adonis autumnalis*

31

The weeds are making their last struggle for the year. Martins congregate in large numbers on roofs. Blackberries ripe.

'Destroy weeds while young: for when they have growen strong and got deep Rooting, they'le not only take the nourishment from the good plant, but there will be such difficulty in grubing them out, that the good seed or plant is in danger of being destroyed; but if you suffer them to bear and sow their seeds, then (besides that they exhaust much more substance of the ground) you shall find the work Intollerable, for they'le poyson the whole ground, insomuch that one year's seeds will cost many years weeding: and therfore prevent these things by keeping doun the weeds; so shall your work become easie and gardens handsome.'
John Reid *The Scots Gard'ner* 1683

SEPTEMBER

signifies seven, was thus called by the Romans,
being the 7th Month from March.
Temperature: 57.1° Fahrenheit (13.9° Celsius).
Rainfall: 2.41 inches (6 cm).

Orpine or Great Live-long, *Sedum telephium*

1

Fasten autumnal flowers and plants to sticks, that may secure them from breaking in violent winds. Barberries ripe.

'In September come Grapes, Apples, Poppies of all colours, Peaches, Melocotones [quince-trees], Nectarines, Cornelians, Wardens [large hard pears], Quinces.'
Francis Bacon *Of Gardens* 1625

'What is still desired and wanted to make the Art of Gardening truly pleasant, familiar, and entertaining, is the Order of Time: To be led, as it were, by the Hand; to be directed and pointed to something to be done, not only each successive Year, but if possible every Day, at least every Month in the Year, towards forwarding the natural Hopes of being rewarded with Fruit and Plenty.'
John Laurence *The Fruit-Garden Kalendar* 1718

Golden Rod, *Solidago*

2

Cow-dung makes a very excellent liquid manure and is very safe in its application; it is best in a fresh state. Hops in flower.

'Fruit gathered too timely, will taste of
    the wood,
will shrink and be bitter, and seldome
    prove good,
So fruit that is shaked, or beat of a tree:
with brusing in falling, soon faultie wil be.

The Barbery, Respis and gooseberry too,
looke now to be planted as other things doo.
The gooseberry, respis and Roses all three:
with strawberries under them, trimly agree.'
Thomas Tusser *Five Hundreth Points of Good Husbandry* 1573

3

Common Yellow Flea-bane, *Inula dystenterica*

1752. Change from the Julian to the Gregorian calendar. Eleven days were dropped and 3 September became 14 September.

'Each orchard now is smiling gay,
Glittering in the morning ray:
Rich clustering plums of varied hue,
Of freckled red and misty blue,
And sun-tanned pears with ruddy streak,
Brown as was summer's lusty cheek.'
John Clare 1793–1864 *The Last of Summer*

4

Pale Pink Soapwort, *Saponaria officinalis*

Let the full crop of onions be now taken up. Yew berries ripe. September is the best month for replanning the borders.

'The great American botanist Asa Gray asked pertinently, and perhaps plaintively, why it was that so many European weeds had become naturalized in America, and so few American weeds in Europe. The pink-flowered Soapwort is one such invader of the USA, with perhaps more to recommend it than some, for the flowers are pretty and fragrant, and the leaves produce a lather and were formerly used by housewives to "scour their treen [wooden] and pewter vessels".'
Alice Coats *The Book of Flowers* 1973

Mushroom or Champignon, *Agaricus campestris*

5

Fungi now abound and to rise and go abroad to gather mushrooms at an early hour in the morning is the occupation of many of the village children.

'I am not an advocate for sowing seeds on a particular day of the week, or month, nor in the full or wane of the moon, nor when the wind blows from the east, west, or any particular point of the compass; these ridiculous and superstitious notions, have been long since, deservedly, banished out of the well informed world; but in this month, above all others in the year, there is an absolute necessity of sowing certain crops, within a few days of particular periods, in order to ensure the best possible success; so that the plants may not become too strong before winter, and, consequently, be subject to start to seed early in spring, previously to their attaining due perfection, nor be too weakly to endure the severities of the ensuing winter.'
Bernard MacMahon *The American Gardener's Calendar* 1806

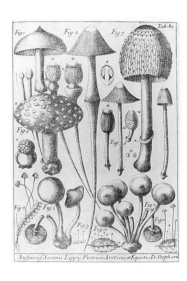

Dandelion, *Leontodon autumnalis*

6

Alexander Neckam born in 1157 in St Albans, Hertfordshire; Abbot of Augustinians, Cirencester 1213; author of *De Naturis Rerum*.

'Vines are loaded with happy fruits, which are composed of good bunches of grapes. In the grape is carried their juice, and when the grape is made into wine, by the genius of nature and the work of agents, helped by the benefit of the warm air, it is happily changed into a most delicious and delightful liquid, and the heart of man is turned to rejoicing.'
Alexander Neckam 1157–1217 *In Praise of Divine Wisdom*

7

Golden Starwort, *Aster solidaginoides*

Spiders generally make some alterations in their webs every twenty-four hours. It has been said, if these changes take place between six and seven o'clock, they indicate a clear and pleasant night.

'Is it not a pleasant sight to behold a multitude of Trees round about: in decent forme and order, bespangled, and gorgeously apparelled with greene Leaves, Bloomes, and goodly Fruits, as with a rich Robe of imbroidered work, or as hanging with some pretious and costly Jewels, or Pearles, the Boughs laden, and burdened bowing downe to you, and freely offering their ripe fruits, as a large satisfaction of all your labours?'
Ralph Austen *A Treatise of Fruit-Trees* 1653

8

Blue Italian Starwort, *Aster amellus*

Take hardwood cuttings. Red admiral butterflies visit scabious flowers.

'The wasps (which are without number this dry hot summer) attack the grapes in a grievous manner. Hung up 16 bottles with treacle, & beer, which makes great havock among them. Bagged about fifty of the best bunches in Crape-bags. Some of the forwardest bunches are very eatable, tho' not curiously ripe.'
Gilbert White *A Garden Kalendar* 1762

Canadian Golden Rod, *Solidago canadenis*

9

Crocuses are obviously suitable for naturalizing in grass, for practically every species blooms in late autumn or early spring, before the grass begins to grow.

'In its way – from the horticultural point of view – September is a gratifying and excellent month; not only because golden rod, autumnal aster, and Indian chrysanthemums are in flower; not only because of you, heavy and amazing dahlias; for know ye, unbelievers, that September is the chosen month for everything that flowers a second time: the month of the second flower; the month of the ripening wine.'
Karel Capek *The Gardener's Year* 1929

Autumnal Crocus, *Crocus autumnalis*

10

5000 working people met in 1844 in the Manchester Free Trade Hall to raise money for public parks.

'The autumn garden…It has its beauty; especially, perhaps, a garden with an old orchard attached to it. When I was very small, about four years old, I suppose, a line of poetry entered into my consciousness, never to leave it again:
     Rye pappels drop about my head.
I had no idea what rye pappels might be, but they held a magic, an enchantment for me, and when in later life I identified them as the ripe apples of Andrew Marvell's poem they had lost nothing of their enchantment in the process of growing up.'
Vita Sackville-West *In Your Garden* 1951

11

Variegated Meadow Saffron, *Colchicum variegatum*

Wasps continue to be very numerous and troublesome, particularly in warm weather. Elderberries ripe.

'Better Saffron groweth not in the world than here in England, being worth forty pounds an acre skilfully and carefully planted, that will last several years, and afford divers crops every year, and must be gathered every morning for a months space.'
Adolphus Speed *Adam out of Eden* 1659

'A fine warm September prolongs the flowering period of many plants which we associate with July and August. Verbenas, Begonias, Geraniums, Cannas, and other half-hardy bedded-out plants are often as bright as ever in September.'
Samuel Graveson *My Villa Garden* 1915

12

Semilunar Passion-flower, *Passiflora peltata*

Potatoes ought now to be dug, provided the haulm is withered. Lime trees commence to shed their leaves.

'Let a Heap of Stones be laid round the Bottom of every new planted Tree: This answers two Purposes; the one is keeping the Earth moist about the Roots, and the other is keeping the Tree steady.'
Martha Bradley *The British Housewife* 1760

'Set out cabbages in the new of the moon to make them head up well, and gather apples in the new of the moon to make them keep well. Plant potatoes in the old of the moon.'
American saying

Officinal Crocus, *Crocus sativus*

13

St Maurilius the Gardener was Bishop of Angers in the fifteenth century, but, overcome with a sense of his unworthiness, went to Britain, where he worked as a gardener. He later returned to Angers, where he died.

'The date of the introduction of saffron (*Crocus sativus*) is unknown, but it was probably introduced by the Romans and as a drug it was well known in Saxon times. It is the only plant that has given a name to a town in these islands – Saffron Walden. In the sixteenth and seventeenth centuries saffron grown in England was accounted the best.'
Eleanour Sinclair Rohde *Shakespeare's Wild Flowers* 1935

Passion-flower, *Passiflora caerulea*

14

The middle of September scarcely ever passes away without sharp frosts. Herald moth appears.

'In the middle ages, the monks in St Bernard's ascetic community at Clairvaux excommunicated a vineyard which a less rigid monk had planted near, so that it bore nothing. In 1120, a bishop of Laon excommunicated the caterpillars in his diocese; and, the following year, St Bernard excommunicated the flies in the Monastery of Foigny; and in 1510 the ecclesiastical court pronounced the dread sentence against the rats of Autun, Macon, and Lyons.'
Charles Dudley Warner *My Summer in a Garden* 1871

15

Byzantine Saffron, *Colchicum byzanticum*

Frances Garnet Wolseley born in 1872 in Dublin; gardening writer who founded the School for Lady Gardeners at Glynde, Sussex 1904.

'Books teach much and so also do lectures, but only when supplemented by practical experience, will they make a competent gardener.'
Frances Wolseley *Gardening for Women* 1908

'No Spring, nor Summer Beauty hath such grace As I have seen in one Autumnall face.'
John Donne 1572–1631 *The Autumnall*

16

Blue Sea Starwort, *Aster tripolium*

Robert Fortune born in 1812 in Edrom, Berwick; plant collector and pioneer in the use of the Wardian case for transplanting plants over long distances; introduced the tea plant from China to India and gave his name to *Fortunella*; Curator of the Chelsea Physic Garden 1846–48.

'When I first discovered the *Anemone japonica*, it was in full flower amongst the graves of the natives, which are round the ramparts of Shanghai; it blooms in November, when other flowers have gone by, and is a most appropriate ornament to the last resting-places of the dead.'
Robert Fortune *Three Years' Wanderings in the Northern Provinces of China* 1847

Narrow-leafed Mallow, *Malva angustiflora*

Working classes celebrated the opening of the Derby Arboretum in 1840, marching with banners to the park. An estimated 9000 people filled the arboretum and not a single tree or shrub was destroyed.

'Good huswives are knowne by their gardens.'
William Ram *Little Dodoen* 1606

'It has been remarked that in September evenings the reduction of temperature begins to be sensibly felt by those who expose themselves to it thinly clad. We cannot concur in the general observation that it is sensibly felt, for the more sensible thing would be to wrap oneself well up, and avoid altogether feeling it.'
Comic Almanac 1835–53

17

Pendulous Starwort, *Aster pendulus*

1840. Children's celebration in the Derby Arboretum, attended by 6000 people.

'September blow soft,
Till fruit be in loft.'
Thomas Tusser *Five Hundreth Points of Good Husbandry* 1573

'The Virginian creeper is turning yellow on the cottage walls, a sure sign of autumn's approach. Old cottages are like illustrated calendars, for you can tell the time of the year by the things that grow on the walls. Quince, vines, roses, jasmine, wistaria, clematis and creepers cling about walls, sills and porches proclaiming the season. There is no need to consult the almanac.'
Patience Strong *The Glory of The Garden* 1947

18

19

Devil's Bit Scabious, *Scabiosa succisa*

Plant spring bulbs. This is a good month in which to sow grass-seed.

'What wond'rous life is this I lead!
Ripe apples drop about my head;
The luscious clusters of a vine
Upon my mouth do crush their wine;
The nectarine, and curious peach,
Into my hands themselves do reach;
Stumbling on melons, as I pass,
Insnared with flowers, I fall on grass.'
Andrew Marvell 1621–78 *The Garden*

20

Common Meadow Saffron, *Colchicum autumnale*

This is of all times of the year the most productive of epidemical disorders of the bowels, which are erroneously ascribed to fruits, but which in reality the autumnal fruits seem best calculated to mollify.

'Oh how sweet and pleasant is the fruit of those trees which a man hath planted and ordered with his owne hand, to gather it and largely and freely bestow and distribute it among his kindred and friends. Above all, let those that have much fruit spare a part to them that have but little or none of their own, and be no niggards but liberate to their neighbours; and this bounty will bring a double blessing, first from God, to increase the fruits; secondly from men, not to diminish them.'
Ralph Austen *A Treatise of Fruit-Trees* 1653

Variegated Fringe-leafed Passion-flower,
Passiflora ciliata

21

**Do not forget to pick honesty that has gone
to seed and hang it up in a dry place until
October.**

'There has fallen a splendid tear
From the passion-flower at the gate.
She is coming, my dove, my dear;
She is coming, my life, my fate;
The red rose cries, "She is near, she is near;"
And the white rose weeps, "She is late;"
The larkspur listens, "I hear, I hear;"
And the lily whispers, "I wait." '
Lewis Carroll *Through the Looking-Glass* 1872

Tree Boletus, *Boletus arbore*

22

**Gather filberts when ripe and store in stone
jars. Swallow and martins begin to depart.
It is hardly possible to have a good flower-
garden where there are a great many hares
and rabbits.**

'Apples be ripe, nuts be brown,
Petticoats up, trousers down.'
Sussex saying

'The invasion of France by the Germans has had
a curious influence on the flora of the former
country. A large number of foreign plants,
chiefly from the South of Europe, the seeds of
which were brought by the invading army along
with forage and by other means, have sprung up
in the neighbourhood of Paris. Two French
botanists have published flora of the two sieges,
including 190 species hitherto unknown to the
district.'
The Cottager's Penny Almanack for 1874

23

White Bushy Starwort, *Aster dumosus*

Apples are now gathered for our English vintage. Mistle thrushes feed on mountain ash berries.

'The delight and pleasure, which by this will arise, will not be small in a little while; when one may behold the waste and wilde places all abounding with fruitfull trees (like the Garden of God) keeping their order, and distance; each one offering the weary traveller some little collation to quench his thirst, and refresh his spirits; inviting him to rest under their shadow, to taste of their delicates, and to spare his purse.'
Samuel Hartlib *A Design for Plentie* 1652

24

Fungus, *Agaricus fimetarius*

Libra: 24 September–23 October. Horace Walpole born in 1717 in London; youngest son of Robert Walpole, Prime Minister; created a garden at Strawberry Hill in Twickenham.

'We have discovered the point of perfection. We have given the true model of gardening to the world; let other countries mimic or corrupt our taste; but let it reign here on its verdant throne, original by its elegant simplicity, and proud of no other art than of softening nature's harshness and copying her graceful touch.'
Horace Walpole *On Modern Gardening* 1770

Great Boletus, *Boletus bovinus*

25

The beauty and lustre of the earth is generally decaying. Ivy in flower. Acorns fall.

'Fungi. Dr Carpenter observes, that the power of expansion which these plants possess, soft as their tissues are, is truly wonderful. Some years ago the town of Basingstoke was paved; and not many months afterwards, the pavement was observed to exhibit an unevenness, which was not easily accounted for. In a short time after, the mystery was explained; for some of the heaviest stones were completely lifted out of their beds by the growth of large toadstools beneath them. One of these stones measured 22 inches by 21, and weighed 83 lbs. It became necessary to re-pave the whole town, in consequence of this remarkable disturbance.' Joseph Harrison *The Gardener's and Naturalist's Almanack for 1853*

Great Golden Rod, *Solidago gigantea*

26

Hazel nuts ready for gathering. Second flowering of honeysuckle.

'It is probably true to say that at no period in history has the cultivation of fruit attracted so much serious attention from householder and scientist as at the present time. Possibly the two major wars of this century did much to force the issue by cutting off supplies from abroad. This had the effect, not only of giving a new lease of life to a rather neglected side of market gardening, but it also drove the ordinary gardener into growing on his own account. Nothing stimulates an industry like shortages and probably at no period in history were so many stocks and fruit trees sold as during the intermediate and post war years of 1940–50.' Frances Perry *The Woman Gardener* 1955

27

North American White and Small-leafed Starwort, *Aster multiflorus*

Autumnal crocus gathered for saffron.

'O Autumn, laden with fruit, and stained
With the blood of the grape, pass not, but sit
Beneath my shady roof; there thou may'st rest,
And tune thy jolly voice to my fresh pipe;
And all the daughters of the year shall dance!
Sing now the lusty song of fruit and flowers.'
William Blake *To Autumn* 1783

28

Evergreen Golden Rod, *Solidago sempervivens*

At the end of September all the tender plants should be taken up or covered up for the winter. Squirrels and dormice collect their winter store.

'The labourer who possesses and delights in the garden appended to his Cottage is generally among the most decent of his class; he is seldom a frequenter of the ale-house; and there are few among them so senseless as not readily to engage in its cultivation when convinced of the comforts and gain derivable from it.'
George Johnson *A History of English Gardening* 1829

Michaelmas Daisy, *Aster tradescanti*

29

Michaelmas. Sunflowers, Michaelmas daisies and dahlias are the flowers of the month. Common snipe and jack snipe arrive.

'A dark Michaelmas
A light Christmas'
Old saying

'It is a good sign that Michaelmas Daisies are gaining in popular attention and favour. When people can admire the comparatively insignificant yet gem-like flowers of the perennial Asters, they are on the road to salvation in matters of floral taste.'
Harry Roberts *The Chronicle of a Cornish Garden* 1901

Golden Amaryllis, *Amaryllis aurea*

30

Edward Hyams born in 1910 in London; garden historian.

'It was perhaps during that half century [1750–1800] that the cottage garden began to become a sort of museum for the old garden flowers, as the landscape garden artists swept out of existence hundreds of old gardens, with their stock of garden plants which had been novelties between 1600 and 1700.'
Edward Hyams *English Cottage Gardens* 1970

OCTOBER

signifies eight, so called by the Romans,
being the 8th Month of their Year.
Temperature: 50° Fahrenheit (10° Celsius).
Rainfall: 2.84 inches (7 cm).

Lowly Amaryllis, *Amaryllis humilis*

1

Once more we are back in the month when the robin sings so much.

'The additional flowers in October are almost confined to the anemone and scabious; and the flowering trees and shrubs to the evergreen cytisus. But the hedges (and here let us observe, that the fields and other walks that are free to every one, are sure to supply us with pleasure, when every other place fails) are now sparkling with their abundant berries – the wild rose with the hip, the hawthorn with the haw, the blackthorn with the sloe, the bramble with the blackberry; and the briony, privet, honey-suckle, elder, holly, and woody night-shade, with their other winter feasts for the birds.'
Leigh Hunt *The Months* 1821

Soapwort, *Saponaria officinalis*

2

Complete all bulb planting as soon as possible. Horse-chestnuts fall.

'In the garden Autumn is, indeed, the crowning glory of the year, bringing us the fruition of months of thought and care and toil. And at no season, save perhaps in Daffodil time, do we get such superb colour effects as from August to November.'
Rose G. Kingsley *The Autumn Garden* 1905

'Many a slovenly slubberdegullion, who is miscalled a cultivator, is in the habit of spoiling good fruit by making it into bad cider.'
Thomas Green Fessenden *The New England Farmer's Almanack for 1828*

3

Downy Helenium, *Helenium pubescens*

Clean up the vegetable garden. Buntings collect in flocks.

'This last week has been sunny and Indian, only the maples along the brookside suggesting the coming of winter. Only a slight frost as yet. The grapes hang temptingly in ripe clusters from the vines, and the apples redden the boughs in the orchards. One is never saturated with sunshine, and tastes the three seasons under the ripened rinds of these fruits.'
Amos Bronson Alcott *Journals* 3 October 1869

4

Dwarf Southernwood, *Artemisia abrotanum*

Pinks and pansies ought to be planted without delay in the beds where they are to bloom.

'Rain may be expected about the 4th, 8th, 15th, 22nd, and 30th of this month. I say it may be expected, but this does not follow that it will come. If it does not, it will fall at some other time, or probably not at all; but the reader may rely upon one or other of these meteorological phenomena taking place.'
Comic Almanac 1835–53

Star-like Chamomile, *Boltonia asteroides*

5

Damsons and bullaces are now fully ripe and are gathered. Both these trees bear immense crops and are used for an excellent conserve, called damson cheese and bullace cheese.

'The White Bullace is worth growing if a spare corner can be found for a tree on account of its excellence and richness when preserved; the preserve will keep a year, and it is particularly luscious and fine-flavoured. The fruit is small and round, and generally grows in pairs. It is yellowish-white when ripe, a little mottled with red on the sunny side, firm and rather acid. The flavour is not very good but it improves when the fruit hangs on the tree until frost touches it, and it is very nice for cooking. It is said to be ripe in October, but it will hang longer. The branches are slender, twiggy, and covered with down.'

Elizabeth Watts *The Orchard and Fruit Garden* 1867

Creeping-rooted Feverfew, *Pyrethrum serotinum*

Cut marrows and bring under cover. Tortoiseshell and peacock butterflies visit ivy flowers.

'This Month you may sow Rhadishes, clear the Alley of all Leafes that have fallen, lest they corrupt and produce, or at least shelter vermin to annoy your Plants and Seeds, and foul your Garden with their Excrements. Prepare covering for tender Herbs and Plants, and be diligent in rectifying what is amiss in every part that your Garden may not be only pleasant and delightful to the eye, but profitable in encrease, by being disencumbered of offensive things.'

Leonard Meager *The Gardener's Almanack* 1697

7

Indian Chrysanthemum, *Chrysanthemum indicum*

Gossamer is still very common in fine weather. Elm leaves turn colour.

'Remove young Plants and Trees in the new of the moon, and about the full of the moon, gather such fruit as you left ungathered the last month; set all kinds of Nuts and Acorns, and cut your Rose trees but once in two years, if you would have store of Roses.'
Poor Robin 1688

'Chrysanthemums are winter favourites. They need summer's forethought and culture, but they grow and flower in winter, and there is something very refreshing in the aromatic smell of these flowers in a season when sweet scents are only thoughts of the past.'
Henrietta Wilson *The Chronicles of a Garden* 1864

8

Sweet Maudlin, *Achillea ageratum*

Wherever you have room plant nut trees, both filbert and hazel. Crabapples fall.

'Plant Gooseberries, Currants, Raspberries and Strawberries, that they may take root before winter; for those which are planted at this season will produce fruit the following summer, whereas those which are planted in spring, have seldom strength enough to produce any (or at least very few) until the second year.'
Philip Miller *The Gardeners Kalendar* 1732

Milky Mushroom, *Agaricus lactifluus acris,* or
A. listeri

9

**Divide and plant out montbretias in open
borders. Female wasps go into hibernation.**

'The question is whether human nature is bad.
We must begin by asking under what
circumstances? Will a peach tree bear peaches?
Yes, if planted in good soil and against a south
wall. Will a rose tree flourish in England? Not if
you set it in an ash-heap and exclude the light
and air. Is a river a beautiful and a wholesome
thing? Yes, when it is fed by the mountain
streams, washed by the autumn rains, and runs
over a pebbly bed, between grassy meadows,
decked with water lilies, fringed with flowering
rushes, shaded by stately trees; but not when it is
polluted by city sewers, stained by the refuse of
filthy dye vats and chemical works.'
Robert Blatchford *Merrie England* 1893

Cape Waved-leafed Aletris, *Aletris viridifolia*

10

**Cuttings of gooseberries and currants can be
inserted in sheltered positions.**

'Then came Autumne all in yellow clad,
As though he joyed in his plentious store,
Laden with fruits that made him laugh, full glad
That he had banisht hunger, which to-fore
Had by the belly oft him pinched sore.'
Edmund Spenser *Faerie Queene* 1611

Common Holly, *Ilex aquifolium*

Leaves of the sumach tree turn yellow and red.

'Holly. Foresight. The providence of Nature demonstrates itself in a singular manner in this handsome plant. Its berries serve to feed the little birds which never quit our climate; and it furnishes them with an hospitable shelter during the rigours of the months of frost. Would it not seem as if Nature, by a tender forethought, had taken pains to preserve the verdure of this fine tree all the winter, and to arm it with thorns in order that it might furnish both food and defence to the innocent creatures that resort to it for refuge? It is a friend which her all-powerful hand preserves against the period when friends fly and all other reliance fails.'
The Language of Flowers 1834

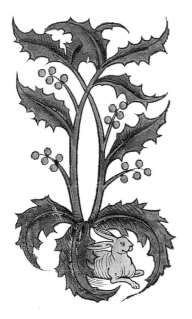

Wavy Fleabane, *Inula undulata*

Butterflies disappear. Ladybird beetles retire to hibernating places.

'Let your owne judgement order your Garden, like your house, and your hearbes like your furniture, placing the best in the best places, and such as are most conspicuous, and the rest according to their dignities in more inferior roomes. From this alligorie, if you can draw any wit, you may finde without my further instruction how to frame Gardens of all sorts to you owne contentment.'
Gervase Markham *The Second Booke of the English Husbandman* 1615

Yellow Smooth Helenium, *Helenium autumnale*

13

Remove dead leaves from rhubarb and place a layer of manure and leaves over the crowns.

'I make no apology for the minuteness with which I shall give my instructions; for my business is *to teach* that which I know; and those who want no teaching, do not want my book. My opinion is, that any man who is so disposed, may become a good gardener by strictly attending to this work.'
William Cobbett *The English Gardener* 1829

Indian Fleabane, *Inula indica*

14

Never have a path for walking on less than three feet wide. Sweet chestnuts ripe.

'I wonder why the autumn turns the great coignetiae vines at Gravetye into such glorious seas of fire, and mine just remains a dull green? There, this afternoon, pergolas and old trees (where the vine had found its way) run with living flame – most beautiful to see. Another love of mine there now is Clematis nutans. This bears myriads of down-dropped flowers, palest yellow, and smelling most deliciously of cowslips. It drapes the door on the east front in perfect beauty, it is so refreshing to find something now, in October, that is in the full pride of life.'
Maude Haworth-Booth *My Garden Diary* 1934

15

Purple Sweet Sultan, *Centaurea moschata*

Autumn, still advancing, gradually diminishes the flowers and leaves, often the later aster and Michaelmas daisy standing up in flower among the dead weeds.

'This is St Luke's summer, or the "Indian summer" as it is called in America. The air is soft and warm and still. The yellow leaves fall from the Beeches in countless numbers, but slowly and noiselessly, and as if reluctant to let go their hold. The rooks come back to us again across the fields, and clamour among the empty nests, which were their homes in spring. The "remontant" Roses are putting out their latest blooms, and the Antirrhinums, Mulleins, and some few other flowers, show themselves "remontant" also. There is an aromatic fragrance everywhere from the withering leaves and from the lingering flowers.'
Henry Arthur Bright *A Year in a Lancashire Garden* 1879

16

Yarrow, *Achillea millefolium*

Make cider and perry of winter fruits throughout this month. Dogwood leaves turn red.

'The general rule for keeping fruit is that storage-rooms should be constructed in a cool, dry place with boarded floors, north-facing windows which are opened on a fine day, and glass windows to keep out the south winds. The draught from a north-east wind also spoils the appearance of pears by shrivelling them. Windfalls should be kept widely spaced. Fruit should have a bed of closely packed straw or chaff and be placed far apart so that the gaps between the rows admit a uniform draught.'
Pliny the Elder AD 23–79 *Natural History*

Dwarf Sunflower, *Helianthus indicus*

17

**Redwings arrive. Give all the specially
delicate plants a good blanket of bracken
before the end of October.**

'Ah, Sun-flower! weary of time,
Who countest the steps of the Sun,
Seeking after that sweet golden clime
Where the traveller's journey is done:

Where the Youth pined away with desire,
And the pale Virgin shrouded in snow
Arise from their graves, and aspire
Where my Sun-flower wishes to go.'
William Blake *Ah! Sun-Flower* 1794

Mushroom, *Agaricus floccosus*

18

**Nicholas Culpeper born in 1616 in London;
radical apothecary and herbalist who
established a medicinal garden in Red Lion
Street, Spitalfields; author of *The English
Physician* 1652.**

'What can be more pleasant to thee, than the
enjoying of Medicines for cure of thine
Infirmities, out of thy Native Soyl, and Countrey,
thy Field, thy Orchard, thy Garden?'
Nicholas Culpeper *The School of Physick* 1659

19

Perennial Tick-seed, *Coreopsis procera*

It is usual that a dry autumn precedes a windy winter; a windy winter, a rainy spring; a rainy spring, a dry summer; a dry summer, a windy autumn.

'Notwithstanding the value which is set upon the Champignon or Mushroom, by Men of polite Taste, and the extraordinary Price which those of the best Sort will bring in the Market; I have not been able to persuade any of our Market Gardeners, to make that Branch of Gardening their Study or Practice.'
Richard Bradley *A General Treatise of Husbandry and Gardening* 1722

20

Yellow Sweet Sultan, *Centaurea suaveolen*

Collections of spiders are best made during this month and the young gardener may continue to dissect and study the pulpy fruits.

'Your fruits should now be gather'd as they ripen; for those which are in eating this month, seldom continue long good: But toward the end of the month most sorts of Winter fruit will be fit to gather; but you should always suffer them to remain as long upon the trees as the weather will permit; for when they are gather'd too early, their skins will shrivel, and the fruit will not keep well; and there will be no danger of their suffering upon the trees until the mornings begin to be frosty, when you must not let the fruit hang longer, because if the frost should pinch their skins, it would greatly injure them. You must always observe to gather your fruit when the trees are perfectly dry, otherwise your fruit will not keep.'
Philip Miller *The Gardeners Kalendar* 1732

Hairy-stalked Silphium, *Silphium asteriscus*

21

The Virginia creeper is particularly rich and beautiful in the autumnal months, with its leaves of every hue, from a bright to a dark green and deep crimson.

'Ah, yet, e'er I descend to th' Grave
May I a small House, and large Garden have!
And a few Friends, and many Books, both true,
Both wise, and both delightful too!'
Abraham Cowley *The Wish* 1647

'The secret of a bright autumn garden is contained in the oft-repeated advice to remove the seed vessels as soon as they are formed from subjects like Pentstemons, Antirrhinums and Violas, and to cut away all weak and useless growth; by this means what is virtually a new flowering plant comes into being.'
Samuel Graveson *My Villa Garden* 1915

Rough Three-leafed Silphium, *Silphium trifoliatum*

22

Phloxes and pentstemons may be planted out in beds this month. Snakes, frogs and toads retire into winter quarters.

'If the season has been very dry, flower-borders may be dug over about the end of the month. Attend, above all things, to neatness. Do not trust to any kalendar for directions in this, or any point; but endeavour to bring your own brain into work, and try to look at your works with the eye of a critic and a stranger, or even of an enemy.'
John Loudon *Encyclopaedia of Gardening* 1822

23

Slender-stalked Starwort, *Aster junceus*

Lift a few roots of mint and plant in boxes, placing the same in a warm house for winter supply.

'The Oil of Rosemary. It hath all the virtues of the oil of cinnamon, nutmegs, caraways, and juniper berries; besides which it is much more powerful than any of them, strengthening the brain and memory, fortifying the heart, resisting poison, and curing all sorts of agues; it is absolutely the greatest strengthener of the sight, and restorer of it also, if lost: it makes the heart merry, and takes away all foolish phantasms out of the brain. It cleanseth the blood, cures tooth-ache, easeth all pains, and takes away the causes which hinder conception: it hath a very grateful taste, and hath so many virtues that I can never express them all, or give it its due commendation.'
Nicholas Culpeper *The English Physician* 1652

24

Carolina Starwort, *Aster carolinus flexuosus*

Scorpio: 25 October–22 November. Marianne North born in 1830 in Hastings, Sussex; travelled round the world and made over 800 paintings of plants.

'Oh roses for the flush of youth,
And laurel for the perfect prime;
But pluck an ivy branch for me
Grown old before my time.

Oh violets for the grave of youth,
And bay for those dead in their prime;
Give me the withered leaves I chose
Before in the old time.'
Christina Rossetti *Song* 1849

Flea-bane Star-wort, *Aster conizoides*

25

The unmistakable smell of autumn is the smell of decay, shot through with the bitter fumes of smoke. Fieldfares arrive.

'One autumn, on the 25th October, I cut from a Vine out of doors a bunch of black Grapes weighing three quarters of a pound, perfectly ripe and covered with bloom; some of the berries were nearly an inch in diameter, and the whole bunch was a very beautiful spectacle. The flavour was delicious. It was taken from a Vine covering about nine square yards, which produced that season nearly a hundred bunches.'
Henry Burgess *The Amateur Gardener* 1854

Late-flowered Golden Rod, *Solidago petiolaris*

26

Snowdrops may be planted in any situation where they can be seen well. Woodcocks arrive.

'Cress is excellent in salads, with lettuces. It is a peppery little thing, far preferable to mustard or rape. It is an annual, and bears prodigious quantities of seed. A small quantity should, in the salad season, be sowed every six days or thereabouts; for it should be cut before it comes into rough leaf. It is sowed in little drills made with the tops of the fingers, and covered slightly with very fine earth: it is up almost immediately, and quite fit to cut in five or six days. This and other small salads may be very conveniently raised, in the winter time, in any hot-bed that you happen to have.'
William Cobbett *The English Gardener* 1829

27

Floribund Starwort, *Aster floribundus*

Tall beeches cast their leaves about the end of October, and feathered thorn moths appear.

'I don't like to see high walls round a garden. There is nothing we need be ashamed of in gardening, and it is well to let passers-by see something of our treasures, whether it is only a small plot in front of a cottage, or a spacious lawn with beds of flowers interspersed. True gardening should breed a spirit of generosity. We interchange seeds and cuttings with our neighbours, and if we are able to send cut flowers to our friends who may not have gardens of their own, we even add to the pleasure we have had in growing the flowers.'
Charles Wyatt *Gardening for Children and Others* 1910

Late-flowering Creeping Chrysanthemum,
Chrysanthemum serotinum

28

**Roll, mow, sweep, hoe, weed and remove
moss and worm-casts. Red admiral butterflies
go into hibernation.**

'Chrysanthemum. Cheerfulness under adversity.
These various coloured flowers cheer us in the
winter and look gay when all is dark and severe.'
Maud Dean *The Language of Flowers* 1897

'It is said that there are still families in Russia,
Germany, England, France, and Italy who are
accustomed to plant a tree at the birth of a child.
The tree, it is hoped, will grow with the child,
and it is tended with special care.'
J. G. Frazer *The Golden Bough* 1890

Autumnal Green Narcissus, *Narcissus viridiflorus*

29

**All plants have a season of rest; discover
what season is peculiar to each and choose
that season for transplanting.**

'The mind of the gardener is, in a way, the mind
of the chess player. He makes a move after
having thought out what the ultimate effect
of that move may be. He visualizes the end
of the game.'
Richardson Wright *The Practical Book of Outdoor
Flowers* 1924

30

Mixen Mushroom, *Agaricus fimetarius*

John Kennedy born in 1759 in Hammersmith, Middlesex; nurseryman who advised the Empress Josephine on her garden at Malmaison, for which he also provided plants in the middle of the Napoleonic Wars.

'This is the time for the domestic cultivator of flowers to finish planting, especially the bulbs that are intended to flower in early spring. And as the chief business of nature this month is dissemination of vegetable birth, so its chief beauty arises from vegetable death. We need not tell our readers we allude to the changing leaves with all their lights and shades of green, amber, red, light red, light and dark green, white, brown, russet, and yellow of all sorts.'
Leigh Hunt *The Months* 1821

31

Fennel-leafed Tick-seed, *Coreopsis ferulaefolia*

John Evelyn born in 1620 in Wotton, Surrey; created a garden at Sayes Court in Deptford; author of *Sylva* 1664.

'The Gardiner should walke about the whole Gardens every Monday-morning duely, not omitting the least corner, and so observe what Flowers or Trees & plants want staking, binding and redressing, watering, or are in danger; especially after great stormes, & high winds and then immediately to reforme, establish, shade, water &c what he finds amisse, before he go about any other work.'
John Evelyn 1620–1706 *Directions for the Gardiner at Says-Court*

NOVEMBER

signifies nine, being the 9th of the Roman Months.
Temperature: 43.5° Fahrenheit (63.9° Celsius).
Rainfall: 2.34 inches (5 cm).

1

Laurustinus, *Laurustinus sempervivens*

All Saints' Day. Whenever an operation directed for one month is left undone, do it as soon as possible.

'November is singularly like early spring. As in March the polyanthus primroses are beginning to flower. The periwinkle and gorse are in full bloom.'
William Beach Thomas *An Observer's Twelvemonth* 1923

'Attend to the grass lawns and verges, sweep up leaves, and pole down wormcasts; turn gravel-walks if weedy or mossy. Take up dahlia roots, and place them secure from frost.'
William Cobbett *The English Gardener* 1829

2

Winter Cherry, *Physalis*

All Souls' Day. Put on winter mulch. A man of words and not of deeds is like a garden full of weeds.

'A soul, a soul, a soul-cake,
Please good missis, a soul-cake.
An apple, a pear, a plum or a cherry,
Any good thing to make us all merry,
One for Peter, two for Paul,
Three for Him who made us all.'
Cheshire song

Primrose, *Primula vulgaris*

3

The cold wet fogs of November now creep on apace and the few flowers remaining in the garden have a melancholy appearance.

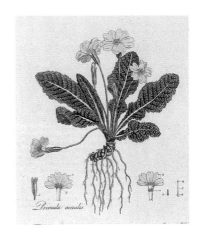

Primula acaulis

'If I had to come into a neglected garden,
I would choose to start my year in November,
for then I should be able to begin working over
the ground at once, and there would be less
temptation to plant for immediate show, and
neglect the due preparation of the soil. All big
changes are best effected in winter – new
borders made and old borders altered, draining
done, ground broken up and manured, rockeries
built, trees planted and paths laid.'
Helena Swanwick *The Small Town Garden* 1907

Strawberry-tree, *Arbutus*

4

The last and latest sorts of our apples and pears are gathered and laid up in the loft at this time.

'In this Month is Arbutus, the Strawberry Tree in
its greatest glory; the body hath a rough but the
branches a smooth Bark, with leaves alternately
green like the Bayes, finely purled about the
edges, long yet round pointed, the flowers grow
on the ends of the branches, with long stalks and
are small little white bottles, like those of the Lilly
of the Valley, which are of little beauty, but
succeeded by red berries like to Straw-berries,
harsh in taste, containing small and many seeds:
the whole rises not here to two yards high, its
usual height in its native Countrey Ireland; the
berries are its beauty, ripe in this Month: and
therefore herein placed, which being mixed with
its fine green leaves, are very delightful to the eye.'
Samuel Gilbert *The Florists Vade-Mecum* 1682

5

Common Winter Cherry, *Physalis alkekengi*

Wind is always by far the worst of the gardener's enemies. Clean tools.

'Thou art a tool of honour in my hands;
I press thee, through the yielding soil, with pride.'
William Wordsworth *To the Spade of a Friend* 1807

'It is chiefly to the autumn leaves that one must
look for colour now – the Japanese Maples, the
Persian Parrotia, Sumach, Azalea, Berberis, and
others; to the fruits the hips and haws of Roses
and Thorns, the berries of Rockspray and
Pernettya, and the Crabs; and to the stems
– of Willow, Dogwood and White Bramble.'
Harry Higgott Thomas *Round the Year in the
Garden* 1916

6

Common Yew Tree of Europe, *Taxus baccata*

**Shrews and field mice go into winter quarters.
It's good practice to mark your seed packets
with the date and their life expectancy the
minute you receive them.**

'This month your melancholy elves
Shoot, poison, drown, and hang themselves;
With some such rage to end her life,
Would heaven might inspire my wife.'
Old Poor Robin's Almanac 1805

Large Furcraea, *Furcraea gigantea*

7

Proceed with the pruning of apple and pear trees, cutting out ill-placed and weak shoots.

'Autumne, the Barber of the yeare, that shaves bushes, hedges, and trees; the ragged prodigall that consumes al and leaves himself nothing; the arrantest beggar amongst al the foure quarters. This bald-pated Autumnus wil be seen walking up and down groves, medows, fields, woods, parks, and pastures, blasting of fruites, and beating leaves from their trees, when common highwayes shall be strewed with boughes in mockery of Summer and in triumph of her death. Then say that Autumne raignes, then is the true falle of the leafe, because the world and the yeare turne over a new leafe.'
Thomas Dekker *Raven's Almanack* 1609

Cape Aletris, *Veltheimia glauca*

8

Grass plots demand attention now. A last mowing should be given them.

'Ice in November to bear a duck,
Nothing after but sludge and muck.'
East Anglian saying

'Gardening, experimental philosophy, and literature, would afford women subjects to think of and matter for conversation, that in some degree would exercise their understandings.'
Mary Wollstonecraft *Vindication of the Rights of Woman* 1792

9

Glaucous-leafed Aletris, *Veltheimia glauca*

Empty pots, that are dirty, should be laid in soak in a tub and cleaned at leisure. Primroses flower in sheltered spots.

'The gardener who imagines that his work can be reduced to a set of rules and formulae, followed and applied according to special days marked on the calendar, is but preparing himself for a double disappointment. Few things are so certain to be uncertain as the seasons and the weather; and these, rather than a set of dates, even for a single locality, form the signs which the real gardener follows. That is the great trouble with much book and magazine gardening.'
Frederick Frye Rockwell *Around the Year in the Garden* 1917

10

Scotch Fir, *Pinus sylvestris*

It is November and the garden has little to offer but beech leaves and chrysanthemums.

'I received today —'s Illustrated Catalogue. I have pored over it all morning and neglected my house. I have no doubt you thought to do me a kindness, but why did you do it? You have upset me, you have unsettled me, you have undone me. You have disinclined me to do my duty strictly in that line of life to which I am called. I want to do the things I can't and I don't want to do the things I have to do. I want to dig and hoe and rake with Paul and water with Appollas and sow and scrape and weed and lay out and set out and pot out and thin out and weed out and bed out and blossom out and *stay out*.'
Catherine Starbuck *Letter from Nantucket* 1879 (*Our Garden Heritage,* ed. Alice Sloane Anderson 1961)

Weymouth Pine, *Pinus strobus*

Feast of St Martin. Golden-crested wrens congregate.

'Go out of doors on a dull November day and sniff the breeze. Brown leaves lie all about you, the garden beds are almost bare, yet the air is full of strange perfumes, stimulating and full of vitality. The tang of bitter-sweet Chrysanthemums is there, the acrid fumes of wood smoke, the rich pungence of trodden Walnut leaves, and now and then one catches a whiff of pure spring, perhaps caught by the breeze from the thready blossoms of the Witch Hazel.'
Louise Beebe Wilder *The Fragrant Path* 1932

11

Great Orange-flowering Aloe, *Veltheimia* or *Aletrisuvaria*

Frost is one of the most potent agents we have for sweetening the land.

'This is the *windy month* of the Saxons; it is generally also cold and moist, and one of the most disagreeable for the labouring gardener, but he may console himself with the shortness of the day, and hail the approach of evening, when he may lay aside his wet dress and fortify his mind by converse with books. Roots, fruits, seeds, dried herbs, and insects require looking over and protecting from damps.'
John Loudon *Encyclopaedia of Gardening* 1822

12

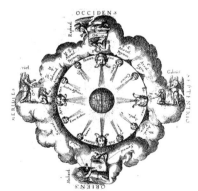

13

Bay, *Laurus poetica*

William Shenstone born in 1714; poet and garden designer; created a 'picturesque' garden at The Leasowes in Warwickshire.

'Apparent art, in its proper province, is always as important as apparent nature. They contrast agreeably; but their provinces ever should be kept distinct.'
William Shenstone *Unconnected Thoughts on Gardening* 1764

'Bay-tree. A bath of the decoction of the leaves and berries is singularly good for women to sit in, that are troubled with the mother, or the diseases thereof, or the stoppings of their courses, or for the diseases of the bladder, pains in the bowels by wind, and stopping of urine.'
Nicholas Culpeper *The English Physician* 1652

14

Portugal Laurel, *Cerasus lusitanica*

Be prepared for a sudden drop in temperature, usually about the end of the second week.

'Portugal Laurels, and Bays, how well they contrast when grown together, both in growth and shade of green – not trimmed shrubbery-walk bushes, but unpruned, uncramped, trees of twenty feet high. The Portugal Laurels, compact and round, with red young wood, footstalks and buds, bright in the sun; and the Bays, wide spreading, on stems from the ground to the topmost waving branch, and separate-growing leaf, contrasting in green colour, especially in the wind, when the light sea green of the back of the leaf is shown with pleasing effect and variety.'
Frances Jane Hope *Notes and Thoughts on Gardens and Woodlands* 1881

Sweet-scented Coltsfoot, *Tussilago fragrans*

15

If you want to leave something behind you that will last for a thousand years and more, plant acorns.

'Montezuma Emperor of Mexico, took a particular Care to transplant into his garden all the choice Simples that benign Climate produced, where the study of the Physicians was to attain to the Knowledge of their Names and Properties. They had Names for all kinds of Pains and Infirmities; and in the Juices and Applications of those Herbs consisted all their remedies, with which they effected surprising cures.'

Robert Colborne *The Plain English Dispensatory* 1753

African Bow-string Hemp, *Sanseviera guineensis*

16

Remake and repair paths and edgings. Wood pigeons collect in large flocks.

'For whatever the land you possess, whether it
      be where sand
And gravel lie barren and dead, or where fruits
      grow heavy
In rich moist ground; whether high on
      steephillside,
Easy ground in the plain or rough among
      sloping valleys –
Wherever it is, your land cannot fail to produce
Its native plants. If you do not let laziness clog
Your labour, if you do not insult with
      misguided efforts
The gardener's multifarious wealth, and if you
      do not
Refuse to harden or dirty your hands in the
      open air
Or to spread whole baskets of dung on the sun-
      parched soil –
Then, you may rest assured, your soil will not
      ail you.'

Walahfrid Strabo *Hortulus* 840

17

Stramony or Thorn-apple Tree, *Datura arborea*

Tulips may be planted out any time during this month.

'There is an old tradition that if red periwinkle is planted outside a garden gate, it is an invitation to the passer-by to come in and look at the garden.' Dorothy Jacob *Flowers in the Garden* 1968

18

Notched leaf Passion-flower, *Passiflora serratifolia*

Honeysuckle berries adorn the hedges. Grey wagtail arrives.

'Winter is striding on, and every bit of colour in the garden becomes more precious than ever. Only a few days ago I made a nosegay of crimson summer Roses, a fine Auratum Lily, a Gladiolus, a Welsh Poppy, and a large red-rimmed annual Poppy, with a wonderful spray of Flexuosa Honeysuckle, that filled the room with its fragrance. A little while since, in one sheltered corner, Salvia Patens still held its own in unsullied blue. Marigolds were plenty; St John's Wort must have made a mistake in its dates, for it was all over polished yellow buds ready to unclose; Mignonette and a few Sweet Peas lingered still.' Mrs Boyle *Days and Hours in a Garden* 1884

Apple-fruited Passion-flower, *Passiflora maliformis*

19

Brimstone and small tortoiseshell butterflies occasionally appear.

'The holly bush, a sober lump of green,
Shines through the leafless shrubs all brown
    and grey,
And smiles at winter be it eer so keen
With all the leafy luxury of May.'
John Clare 1793–1864 *Winter Walk*

Red Stapelia, *Stapelia rubra*

20

Arches, pergolas and other erections for climbing plants should be made now so as to give them time to settle before planting.

'In Winter time, if you cover the grounde which you meane to breake up in the Spring, with good store of Ferne, it keepeth down grass and weeds from springing up in Winter, which wold spend some part of the heart of the ground, and it dooth also enrich the ground mightily, for all maner of rootes and hearbs. Ashes of ferne are excellent.'
Hugh Platt *Floraes Paradise* 1608

21

Wood Sorrel, *Oxalis grandiflora*

Asters and such like plants are often checked in their growth and flowering by frosts and rains; attend to them, as they are apt to be blown about and disfigured at this season.

'When George Eliot went to Stratford-on-Avon she was given a sprig of rosemary, from a bush said to have been there in Shakespeare's day. She took it back to Wimbledon and planted it herself in her garden. Mr Trower was given a slip from this bush, which he, like George Eliot, planted himself, and he was kind enough to give me a slip from the bush. I in turn carefully planted it, and when large enough I will joyfully give slips to anyone who cares for them.'
Eleanour Sinclair Rohde *The Scented Garden* 1931

OXALIS scapo unifiore,
foliis ternatis, radice bulbosa. *Hort. Cliff.*

22

Tube-flowered Wood Sorrel, *Oxalis tubiflora*

The thread of the spider is so fine that two drachms [an eighth of an ounce] in weight would reach from London to Edinburgh, or a distance of 400 miles.

'Ivy berries afford a noble and providential supply for birds in winter and spring; for the first severe frost freezes and spoils all the haws, sometimes by the middle of November. Ivy berries do not seem to freeze.'
Gilbert White *The Natural History of Selborne* 1768–92

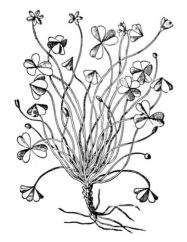

Convex Sorrel, *Oxalis convexula*

23

**Sagittarius: 23 November–21 December.
Titmice frequent gardens.**

'A very interesting, small winter flower garden
may be formed by planting a plot of ground
principally with hardy evergreen shrubs, which,
how sombre soever they may look during
summer, when all around is blooming, yet,
during winter cannot fail to give rise to pleasing
associations by their verdure and clothing when
the flower beds were naked and bare. The shrubs
best adapted to this purpose, are arbutuses,
andromedias, arborvitois, brooms, Spanish and
Portugal, hollies, kalmias, laurels of sorts,
mahonias, rhododendrons, lauristenuses, and
heaths.'
Robert Adamson *The Cottage Garden* 1856

Starry Stapelia, *Stapelia radiata*

24

**Hardy climbers may at once be pruned and
trained. Winter and mottled umber moths
appear.**

'Opinions differ as to what kind of wood is
best for fuel. Pine wood burns freely, from the
quantity of turpentine it contains, but it does
not give out much heat. Beech is preferred on
the continent of Europe, and maple in
America; but Count Rumford says that the
greatest mass of radiant heat is produced by the
fuel of the lime tree. Generally speaking, close-
grained smooth woods make better fuel than
those the grain of which is open and rough.'
Jane Loudon *The Lady's Country Companion* 1845

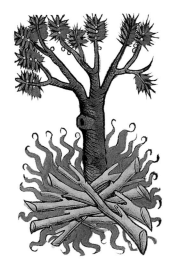

25

Sweet Butterbur, *Tussilago fragrans*

Blossoms on the gorse. Greenfinches assemble in flocks.

'Still – look forward hopefully as we will, work cheerily on as we may, and enjoy as we can and ought the many beauties that autumn brings – her bright, clear days, the brilliant colouring of tree and shrub, the rich array of scarlet berries on rowan, rose, and hawthorn – still, there is no denying that, late in autumn, our hearts feel saddened at the decay around us, and most people feel it a season of pensive retrospect rather than of cheerful looking forward.'
Henrietta Wilson *The Chronicles of a Garden* 1864

26

Linear Sorrel, *Oxalis linearis*

A final hoeing will clear the ground of weeds before the spring bulbs begin to shoot and make hoeing difficult.

'There is nothing like gardening to keep one young. It is the most rejuvenating of all occupations. One is always looking forward to next year, or five years hence.'
Vita Sackville-West *The Observer* 26 November 1950

'There is yet one thing to notice in this laying-out of the garden; namely, that there must be a *shed* to serve as a place for depositing tools, flower-pots, and the like; and also, for the gardeners to retire to in case of rain, and to do works there when they cannot do work out of doors.'
William Cobbett *The English Gardener* 1829

Lupin-leafed Sorrel, *Oxalis lupinifolia*

**November generally proves a dirty month,
the earth and trees wholly unclothed.**

'The trees generally lose their leaves in the
following succession: walnut, mulberry, horse-
chestnut, sycamore, lime, ash; then, after an
interval, elm; then beech and oak; then apple and
peach trees, sometimes not till the end of
November; and lastly oaks and young beeches,
which retain their withered leaves till pushed off
by their new ones in spring.'
Leigh Hunt *The Months* 1821

27

Variegated Stapelia, *Stapelia variegata*

**Dreary, dark November is made cheerful with
the varied, chaste, and brilliant colours of the
chrysanthemum.**

'Summer was dead and Autumn was expiring,
And infant Winter laughed upon the land
All cloudlessly and cold; when I, desiring
More in this world than any understand,
Wept o'er the beauty, which, like sea retiring,
Had left the earth bare as the wave-worn sand
Of my lorn heart, and o'er the grass and flowers
Pale for the falsehood of the flattering Hours.'
Percy Bysshe Shelley *The Zucca* 1822

28

29

Sphenogyne, *Sphenogyne piliflora*

Gertrude Jekyll born in 1843 in London; gardening writer and designer who pioneered the modern informal style of gardening.

'Those who do not know are apt to think that hardy flower gardening of the best kind is easy. It is not easy at all. It has taken me half a lifetime merely to find out what is best worth doing, and a good slice of another to puzzle out ways of doing it.'

Gertrude Jekyll *Colour in the Flower Garden* 1908

30

Three-colored Sorrel, *Oxalis tricolor*

St Andrew's Day. The Order of the Thistle was instituted by Achaius of Scotland in 787, restored by James V in 1540, revived by King James II in 1687, and reestablished by Queen Anne in 1703.

'The Scotch Thistle, although possessing no beauty of flower, is remarkable for its size and stately appearance; which in the open border, in favourable situations, will attain a height of eight or nine feet, with leaves three or four feet in length. The plant is not only ornamental but useful, as the old stems will make handsome walking-sticks; and as they are hollow, they may be applied to different useful purposes.'

Joseph Harrison *The Gardener's and Naturalist's Almanack for 1853*

'Today we bid adieu to the gloomy month of November, which so many of the Dutch and English dread as the month of suicidal dullness and mental despondency.'

Circle of the Seasons 1828

DECEMBER

signifies the 10th Month in the Roman Year,
and was dedicated by them to Saturn.
Temperature: 39.9° Fahrenheit (4.4° Celsius).
Rainfall: 2 inches (5 cm).

1

Dark Stapelia, *Stapelia pulla*

The earth is generally fast locked up under its frozen coat, that the husbandman hath leisure to sit and spend what store he hath before-hand provided.

'My garden is all covered up by snow; picked gilliflower Tuesday, now gillyflowers are asleep. The hills take off their purple frocks, and dress in long white nightgowns.'
Emily Dickinson *Letters* December 1861

'December. We daily pick pansies and sweet-scented violets, with good long stems, and only wish that the few pale primulas would not nestle so very closely into the fat leaves. Even the polyanthus roses are still in flower here and there.'
William Beach Thomas *An Observer's Twelvemonth* 1923

2

Lemon Geodorum, *Geodorum citrinum*

Deep digging is the best kind of fertilizer, as it allows frost and rain to break up soil particles.

'December is not the month for the full enjoyment of the garden; it is the month of pleasant memories, and it may be also of pleasant anticipations. By this I mean that a good gardener, as he looks round his trees and shrubs, and even his herbaceous plants, can form a fairly true estimate of his prospects for the coming year.'
Canon Ellacombe *In a Gloucestershire Garden* 1895

'Reading is good but the garden is the best teacher.'
Christine Allison *365 Days of Gardening* 1995

Indian Tree, *Euphorbia tirucalli*

3

**This month you may dig up liquorice.
Plant mint in boxes for forcing.**

'Keep the green-house close against the piercing colds. Turne and refresh your fruit in a clear serene day. Sharpen and mend tools. Gather oziers and hassell Rods and make baskets in stormy weather. Cover your water pipes with leitter lest the frosts do crak them, feed weak bees.'
John Reid *The Scots Gard'ner* 1683

'Don't garden only in spring and summer. The most important work to be done in the garden takes place between the months of September and April, and, unless this work is done, the wonderful summer show for which you hope, will never materialize.'
Edward R. Anson *The Owner Gardener* 1934

Barbados Gooseberry, *Cactus pereskia*

4

Plants, tools and gardening books make pleasant Christmas presents and breed good fellowship among gardeners.

'Books alone, however well written, or richly stored with facts, cannot teach all that is necessary to be known about the subject; they can only act as a guide. Hence it is that during the present month we must examine the work of the past, and note down errors of practice that have led to failures for rectification; so as to go forward with additional experience and a firm resolve to merit success in the new year.'
T. W. Saunders *The Garden Calendar* 1887

5

Long-stalked Hibiscus, *Hibiscus pedunculatus*

Samuel Reynolds Hole born in 1819 in Ardwick, Manchester; Dean of Rochester and first President of the National Rose Society; author of *A Book About Roses* 1869.

'Perhaps the best relaxation for December is to turn to the gardening books and catalogues, which provide much food for reflection and tell many fairy tales. It is fairly safe when you read of a scarlet flower to expect only a red one; to translate orange as yellow, yellow as primrose, mauve as lavender, crimson as dark red, and so on, and to regard with suspicion the flowers of purplish-rose.'
Harry Higgott Thomas *Round the Year in the Garden* 1916

6

Nest-flowered Heath, *Erica nudiflora*

Hilda Winifred Ivy Leyel born in 1880 in Uppingham, Rutland; founded the Society of Herbalists in 1927 and edited Mrs Grieve's *Modern Herbal* in 1931.

'Surely it makes a garden more romantic and wonderful to know that Wallflowers, Irises, Lupins, Delphiniums, Columbines, Dahlias and Chrysanthemums, every flower in the garden from the first Snowdrop to the Christmas Rose, are not only there for man's pleasure but have their compassionate use in his pain.'
Hilda Leyel *Modern Herbal* 1931

Hairy Achania, *Achania pilosa*

The natural commencement of the winter season. Yellowhammers congregate.

7

'In this Month little can be expected to be done as to Gardening, and therefore may be termed to the careful Gardener a Month of Rest, wherein he ought to take care of himself in providing wholsome, nourishing Diet, warm Cloaths and good Fires; yet let him look after such things as yet require his Care, especially in the Green-house, or Conservatory, which now will prove an easie Task, the main being to keep the Windows and Doors well closed, and lined with Matts or other Conveniences, to prevent the piercing Air entering through Crevices; for now the Orange-trees are most likely to be in danger, and therefore if the Weather be extream, assist them with the kindly heat of Fire, but not too much, for that does more harm than cold.'
Leonard Meager *The Gardener's Almanack* 1697

American Arbor Vitae, *Thuja occidentalis*

Luminous centipedes appear on banks. Liverwort abundant in gardens.

8

'The winter of 1848 and 1849 will be a season of awful suffering among the labouring classes, unless they are employed, and therefore it behoves every gentleman who can improve his estate by labour, to engage it by all means. A whole village may be saved from incalculable suffering, by the engagement of a few labourers through the winter.'
George Glenny *Garden Almanac for 1849*

9

Corsican Spruce, *Pinus Laricio*

**The *Spectator* very wisely recommends
a winter garden, composed of evergreens,
hedges of holy yew and box, the pyracantha
and other evergreens, whose berries ornament
our hibernal gardens; and the trees might be
pines, firs, cedars and cypress.**

'The under gardeners, though necessarily hardy,
and the open air is their appropriate
whereabouts, should have work assigned to
them appropriate to the clemency or inclemency
of the season; for no men are more liable to
suffer early in life from rheumatism.'
George Johnson *The Cottage Gardener's Dictionary*
1852

10

Portugal Cypress, *Cupressus pendula*

**It is a good idea to keep a garden notebook,
so that successes and failures can be
recorded.**

'In some seasons there is no difficulty in
making a bouquet in December. One year,
on the 10th of the month, we gathered, in good
condition, flowers enough to fill several vases
and baskets, among them being China Roses,
Phlox Drummondi, Verbena, Mignonette,
Erysium, with its deep orange spikes, and
Chrysanthemums; besides Laurustinus, Holly,
and other Evergreens. I must not omit to add
some beautiful Primroses, and an abundance
of fine blooms of the Helleborus niger, or
Christmas Rose.'
Henry Burgess *The Amateur Gardener* 1854

Aleppo Pine, *Pinus halepensis*

If you wish to have window boxes, these should be prepared in the winter.

'The Recess which this Month affords, gives also an Opportunity to the inquisitive Naturalist to make use of his Microscope within Doors; whereby he is assisted to discover those numberless Eggs of little Animals, lodg'd in the Root, the Bark, the leaves, and tender Branches of Trees. These being the devouring Enemies of vegetable Nature, and the Cause of many of those Blights which bring Grief and Disappointment to the most industrious, he first discovers, and then destroys them in their Embrio's.'
John Laurence *The Fruit-Garden Kalendar* 1718

11

Crowded Heath, *Erica abietina*

Protect globe artichokes from frost by covering them with ashes to a depth of ten inches.

'Sometimes a comrade is ill, and a few flowers go to cheer him; whilst parents and teachers are not forgotten by the little ones in the distribution of their gifts. On one occasion, during some very cold weather, we were able to invite fourteen of our children, who happened to be very poor, to a "feast" of boiled potatoes and butter. The potatoes had been grown in our own garden. All the preparations for the "feast" – the washing and boiling of the potatoes, the setting of the tables, etc., were made by small groups of children, who afterwards saw also to the clearing and washing up of the plates and spoons, etc.'
Lucy Latter *School Gardening* 1906

12

13

African Arbor Vitae, *Thuja cupressoides*

The delicious Chimomanthus fragrans (winter sweet), which does best on a south or west wall, begins to flower in December.

'Winter is come, that blowes the balefull breath,
And after winter commeth timely death.'
Edmund Spenser *The Shepheards Calendar* 1611

14

Swamp Pine, *Pinus palustris*

At Bayswater, on 14 December 1843, died John Claudius Loudon, one of the most voluminous and judicious of modern horticultural and botanical writers.

'Landscape-Gardening is practised in the United States on a comparatively limited scale; because, in a country where all men have equal rights, and where every man, however humble, has a house and garden of his own, it is not likely that there should be many large parks.'
John Loudon *Encyclopaedia of Gardening* 1822

Pitch pine, *Pinus resinosa*

If the ground can be dug in December, making a rock garden is splendid winter work.

'Now fire and hot meates have thou must,
December loves warme potions.
Drink wine, beware of too much lust:
Goe warme and use strong motions.'
William Ram *Little Dodoen* 1606

15

Chinese Arbor Vitae, *Thuja orientalis*

During heavy falls of snow, many choice evergreens and ornamental shrubs may suffer damage. It is advisable to shake them free of snow whenever possible.

'This month (the days being at the shortest) is the darkest of the whole year, and is subject to different sorts of weather, sometimes the ground is frozen up, so that little can be done in the garden; and at other times there are hard rains, and thick stinking fogs, which render it very uncomfortable stirring abroad, and are very injurious to tender plants.'
Philip Miller *The Gardeners Kalendar* 1732

16

17

White Cedar, *Cupressus thyoides*

Wooden seed-boxes can be repaired and thoroughly cleaned, for use later.

'Beechwood fires are bright and clear
If the logs are kept a year.
Chestnut only good they say,
If for long 'tis laid away.
Birch and fir logs burn too fast,
Blaze up bright and do not last.
It is by the Irish said
Hawthorn bakes the sweetest bread.
Elm wood burns like churchyard mould,
E'en the very flames are cold.
Poplar gives a bitter smoke,
Fills your eyes and makes you choke.
Apple wood will scent your room,
With an incense like perfume.
Oak and maple, if dry and old,
Keep away the winter's cold.
But ash wood wet or ash wood dry,
A king shall warm his slippers by.'
Anon

18

New Holland Cypress, *Cupressus australis*

Wonderful bark colour-schemes can be worked out in the December garden.

'Some I confess there are that value not much
a Winter Garden, nor care that their flowers
should come too early in the Spring, because
they dare not venture into their Gardens to take
the pleasure of them before the weather be
grown warmer.'
Robert Sharrock *An Improvement to the Art of
Gardening* 1694

'Winter is known by frost and snow,
To all the little girls and boys;
But its enough for me to know,
I get no greens except savoys.'
Poor Robin 1808

Two-coloured Heath, *Erica bicolor*

19

**A tool-shed is the potterer's paradise.
Groundsel flowering in sheltered places.**

'The winter-flowering heathers thrive mightily
in this damp peaty soil. There is something
about heather that brings a whiff of the wide
open spaces that lie beyond the garden. It is
a good all-the-year-round plant for the garden-
maker to remember when he is wondering what
to do with an odd bit of ground.'
Patience Strong *The Glory of the Garden* 1947

Stone Pine, *Pinus pinea*

20

**Daisy flowering on lawns. If we wish to force
any of our rhubarb we must start to do so in
December.**

'For five or six months in the winter I live in
London. People often envy me this, and say:
"What could you do in the garden in the
winter?" But no true gardener would make this
remark, as there is much to be done at all times
and seasons. Half the interest of a garden is the
constant exercise of the imagination. You are
always living three, or indeed six, months hence.
I believe that people entirely devoid of
imagination never can be really good gardeners.
To be content with the present, and not striving
about the future, is fatal.'
Mrs Earle *Pot-Pourri from a Surrey Garden* 1897

21

Sparrow-wort, *Erica passerina*

Shortest day. The China roses are with us still and, under proper management, will stay with us till the snowdrops come.

'So in December the garden is mostly found in a great number of garden catalogues. The gardener himself hibernates under glass in a heated room, buried up to the neck, not in manure or brushwood, but in garden catalogues and circulars, books and pamphlets.'
Karel Capek *The Gardener's Year* 1929

22

Pellucid Heath, *Erica pellucida*

Capricorn: 22 December–20 January. Common chickweed occasionally flowers.

'With holly and ivy,
So green and so gay,
We deck up our houses
As fresh as the day,
With bays, and rosemary,
And laurel complete;
And every one now
Is a king in conceit.'
Poor Robin's Almanac 1695

Cedar of Lebanon, *Pinus cedrus*

All vegetables of our climate seem now to sleep; the days are short and every little warmth from the sun makes every curious lover of gardens wish for the spring.

'Gilt holly, with its thorny pricks,
And yew and box, with berries small,
These deck the unused candlesticks,
And pictures hanging by the wall.'
John Clare *The Shepherd's Calendar* 1827

23

Frankincense Pine, *Pinus taeda*

Cider used to be poured over the roots of apples as a libation and the poet Herrick records the custom of drinking to the health of all fruit trees on Christmas Eve:

'For more or less fruits they will bring
As you give them wassailing.'

'If the birds pipe afore Christmas they'll greet [weep] after.'
Scottish saying

24

25

Holly, *Ilex aculeata baccifera*

Cocks crow most in still weather and before rain; they crow much about Christmas.

'Cover such herbs as cannot abide cold and hard winter, with Fearne or straw, and God send a merrie Christmas.'
William Ram *Little Dodoen* 1606

'At Christmas I no more desire a rose
Than wish a snow in May's new fangled earth;
But like of each thing that in season grows.'
William Shakespeare *Love's Labour's Lost* 1590

26

Purple Heath, *Erica purpurea*

Mistletoe, sacred to the Druids, has for centuries been used to decorate homes at Christmas. Time spent in careful planning now will save much time later on.

'The woods were in their winter sleep,
Rocked in that repose divine
On the wind-swept Apennine;
And dreaming, some of Autumn past,
And some of Spring approaching fast,
And some of April buds and showers,
And some of songs in July bowers,
And all of love.'
Percy Bysshe Shelley *With a Guitar, to Jane* 1822

Flame Heath, *Erica flammea*

27

You must be very careful to keep the frost out of the room where you keep your choice winter fruit, for whenever any of the fruit are frozen, they certainly decay soon after.

'In the small garden perhaps the herbaceous borders still hold pride of place, but in larger gardens, where the cost of maintaining large herbaceous borders is a consideration, the flowering shrub is being planted in increasing numbers. Possibly the only form of gardening which seems to be coming into favour purely on its merits is the Heath Garden. Gardeners have been slow to recognise the fact that, with judicious selection, heaths may be had in flower practically the whole year round.'
The Gardener's Year Book 1927

Bloody-flowered Heath, *Erica cruenta*

28

Examine your orchards and cut all dead branches out of the trees, as also such as cross each other.

'The most noteworthy thing about gardeners is that they are always optimistic, always enterprising, and never satisfied. They are forever planting, and for ever digging up. They always look forward to doing better than they have ever done before. "Next year…" they say, and even as they pronounce the words you become infected by their enthusiasm, and allow yourself to be persuaded that the garden will indeed look different, quite different, next year. Experience tells you that it never does; but how poor and disheartening a thing is experience compared with hope! Let us continue to be sanguine even at the cost of future disillusionment.'
Vita Sackville-West *Country Notes* 1939

29

Heath, *Erica genistopha*

Common gorse flowering. Great, blue, coal and marsh titmice visit gardens.

'In the afternoon I moon about with Vita trying to convince her that planning is an element in gardening. I want to show her that the top of the moat-walk must be planted with forethought and design. She wishes just to jab in the things which she has left over. The tragedy of the romantic temperament is that it dislikes form so much that it ignores the effect of masses. She wants to put in stuff which "will give a lovely red colour in autumn". I wish to put in stuff which will furnish shape to the perspective. In the end we part, not as friends.'
Harold Nicolson *Diaries* 1946

30

Glandular Ponthieva, *Ponthieva glandulosa*

Prepare your next year's seed list.

'My philistine of a husband often told with amusement how a cousin when asked when he expected to finish his garden replied, "Never, I hope." And that, I think, applies to all true gardeners.'
Margery Fish *We Made A Garden* 1956

31

'There is no flower appropriated to the 31st
December.'
William Hone *The Every-Day Book* 1826

The fragrant wallflower still flowers.

'If New Year's Eve night-wind blow *south*,
It betokeneth warmth and growth;
If *west*, much milk and fish in the sea;
If *north*, much cold and storms there will be;
If *east*, the trees will bear much fruit;
If *north-east*, flee it man and brute!'
Anon

'May your flowers flourish, your bees prosper,
your birds love you, and your pet fishes live
for ever. May the blight never visit the tendrils
that make your arbours and porches leafy,
your borders gay, or your fern-banks
verdurous; and may you find in every little
thing that lives and grows a pleasure for the
present hour, and a suggestion of things
higher and brighter for contemplation in the
future. I herein reach my hand towards you
with an affectionate FAREWELL!'
Shirley Hibberd *Rustic Adornments for Homes of
Taste* 1865